DK Kids' First
SCIENCE
BOOK

JACK CHALLONER
AND ANGELA WILKES

DK

DORLING KINDERSLEY
LONDON • NEW YORK • MOSCOW • SYDNEY
www.dk.com

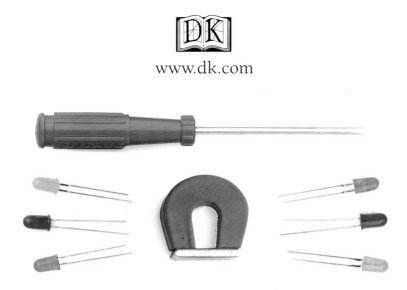

DK

www.dk.com

Design Penny Lamprell and Thomas Keenes
Editor Helen Drew
Production Norina Bremner
Managing Editor Jane Yorke
Managing Art Editors
Chris Scollen and Roger Priddy

Photography Dave King
Illustrations Brian Delf

Published in Great Britain by
Dorling Kindersley Limited,
9 Henrietta Street,
London WC2E 8PS

2 4 6 8 10 9 7 5 3 1

Projects originally published by Dorling Kindersley in
My First Science Book (published 1990, reprinted 1990 twice,
1991, 1992 with revisions, 1995, and 1996) and
My First Batteries & Magnets Book (published 1992, reprinted 1994)

Copyright © 1990, 1992, 1999
Dorling Kindersley Limited, London

A CIP catalogue record for this book is
available from the British Library.

ISBN 0-7513-6634-X

Colour reproduction by Colourscan, Singapore
Printed and bound in Italy by L.E.G.O.

Dorling Kindersley would like to thank
Michelle Baxter, Jonathan Buckley, Jane Bull,
Amy Douglas, Mandy Earey, Nancy Graham,
Westley Kirton, Steve Parker, Peter Radcliffe,
Dawn Sirett and Toby Spigel for their
help in producing this book.

CONTENTS

SCIENCE BY PICTURES

DK Kid's First Science Book is full of fascinating experiments to do at home that will help you to find out more about why things happen the way they do in the world around you. Step-by-step photographs and simple instructions tell you exactly what to do, and there are life-size photographs of everything you need to collect and of the finished projects. Below are the points to look for on each page when using this book and on the opposite page is a list of important things to remember.

How to use this book

The aim of the experiment
The introduction to each project tells you important information and sets out the aim of each experiment.

The things you need
The things to collect for each experiment are shown life-size, to help you check you have everything you need.

Equipment
The illustrated checklists show you which equipment to have ready before you start an experiment.

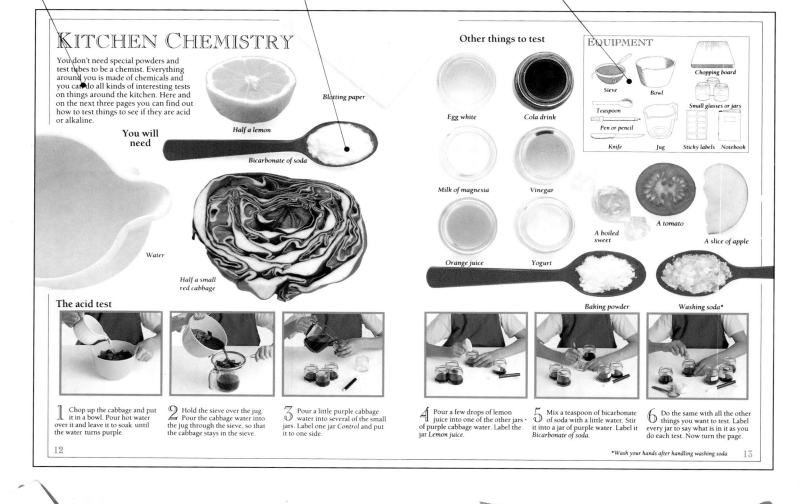

KITCHEN CHEMISTRY

You don't need special powders and test tubes to be a chemist. Everything around you is made of chemicals and you can do all kinds of interesting tests on things around the kitchen. Here and on the next three pages you can find out how to test things to see if they are acid or alkaline.

You will need

Blotting paper

Half a lemon

Bicarbonate of soda

Water

Half a small red cabbage

Other things to test

Egg white

Cola drink

Milk of magnesia

Vinegar

A tomato

A boiled sweet

A slice of apple

Orange juice

Yogurt

Baking powder

Washing soda*

EQUIPMENT

Sieve

Bowl

Chopping board

Teaspoon

Small glasses or jars

Pen or pencil

Knife

Jug

Sticky labels

Notebook

The acid test

1 Chop up the cabbage and put it in a bowl. Pour hot water over it and leave it to soak until the water turns purple.

2 Hold the sieve over the jug. Pour the cabbage water into the jug through the sieve, so that the cabbage stays in the sieve.

3 Pour a little purple cabbage water into several of the small jars. Label one jar *Control* and put it to one side.

4 Pour a few drops of lemon juice into one of the other jars of purple cabbage water. Label the jar *Lemon juice*.

5 Mix a teaspoon of bicarbonate of soda with a little water. Stir it into a jar of purple water. Label it *Bicarbonate of soda*.

6 Do the same with all the other things you want to test. Label every jar to say what is in it as you do each test. Now turn the page.

12

*Wash your hands after handling washing soda 13

Things to remember

1 For projects requiring electricity, use only batteries. **Never use electricity from the wall sockets because it is very dangerous.**

2 Be very careful when using scissors, wire strippers and screwdrivers. **Do not use them unless an adult is with you and always ask an adult to help you make holes through card.**

3 Put on an apron and cover your work area with newspaper before you start.

4 Read all the instructions before you begin each experiment and gather together everything you will need.

5 Keep a science notebook for recording the experiments and your results.

6 Turn off battery-powered projects when you are not using them because batteries may get hot, or run down.

7 When you have finished, put everything away, clean up any mess and wash your hands.

Step-by-step instructions
Step-by-step photographs and clear instructions tell you exactly what to do at each stage of the experiment.

Useful explanations
Clear and simple explanations at the end of experiments tell you what has happened and why.

The final results
Life-size pictures show you what happens in each experiment, and what the finished project looks like.

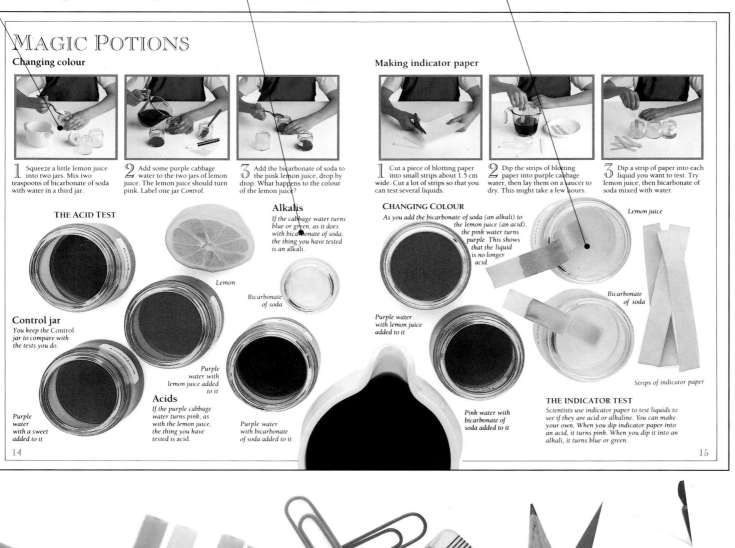

MAGIC POTIONS

Changing colour

1 Squeeze a little lemon juice into two jars. Mix two teaspoons of bicarbonate of soda with water in a third jar.

2 Add some purple cabbage water to the two jars of lemon juice. The lemon juice should turn pink. Label one jar *Control*.

3 Add the bicarbonate of soda to the pink lemon juice, drop by drop. What happens to the colour of the lemon juice?

THE ACID TEST

Alkalis
If the cabbage water turns blue or green, as it does with bicarbonate of soda, the thing you have tested is an alkali.

Lemon

Bicarbonate of soda

Control jar
You keep the Control jar to compare with the tests you do.

Purple water with lemon juice added to it

Acids
If the purple cabbage water turns pink, as with the lemon juice, the thing you have tested is acid.

Purple water with a sweet added to it

Purple water with bicarbonate of soda added to it

Making indicator paper

1 Cut a piece of blotting paper into small strips about 1.5 cm wide. Cut a lot of strips so that you can test several liquids.

2 Dip the strips of blotting paper into purple cabbage water, then lay them on a saucer to dry. This might take a few hours.

3 Dip a strip of paper into each liquid you want to test. Try lemon juice, then bicarbonate of soda mixed with water.

CHANGING COLOUR
As you add the bicarbonate of soda (an alkali) to the lemon juice (an acid), the pink water turns purple. This shows that the liquid is no longer acid.

Lemon juice

Purple water with lemon juice added to it

Pink water with bicarbonate of soda added to it

Bicarbonate of soda

Strips of indicator paper

THE INDICATOR TEST
Scientists use indicator paper to test liquids to see if they are acid or alkaline. You can make your own. When you dip indicator paper into an acid, it turns pink. When you dip it into an alkali, it turns blue or green.

14

15

SCIENCE KIT

Here you can see the equipment you will need to do the experiments in this book. Page 80 has lots of tips on where to buy these things.

Batteries, bulbs and electronic components come in many sizes, so be careful to buy the right ones. Other useful things for your kit include: glue, jars, string, food colouring, a torch, a magnifying glass, a pencil, a notebook, sticky labels, a ruler and paper towels.

A 9V (9 Volt) battery

A 1.5V battery

A 4.5V battery

Small electric motors (1.5V-4V)

1.5V, 2.5V, 3.5V and 4.5V bulbs

Bulb holders

A variable resistor

Electronic components for the transistor radio (see pages 74-75)

LEDs (Light Emitting Diodes)

Wire strippers

Pliers

Lots of plastic-coated flex

An earphone for radio (sometimes called a crystal earpiece)

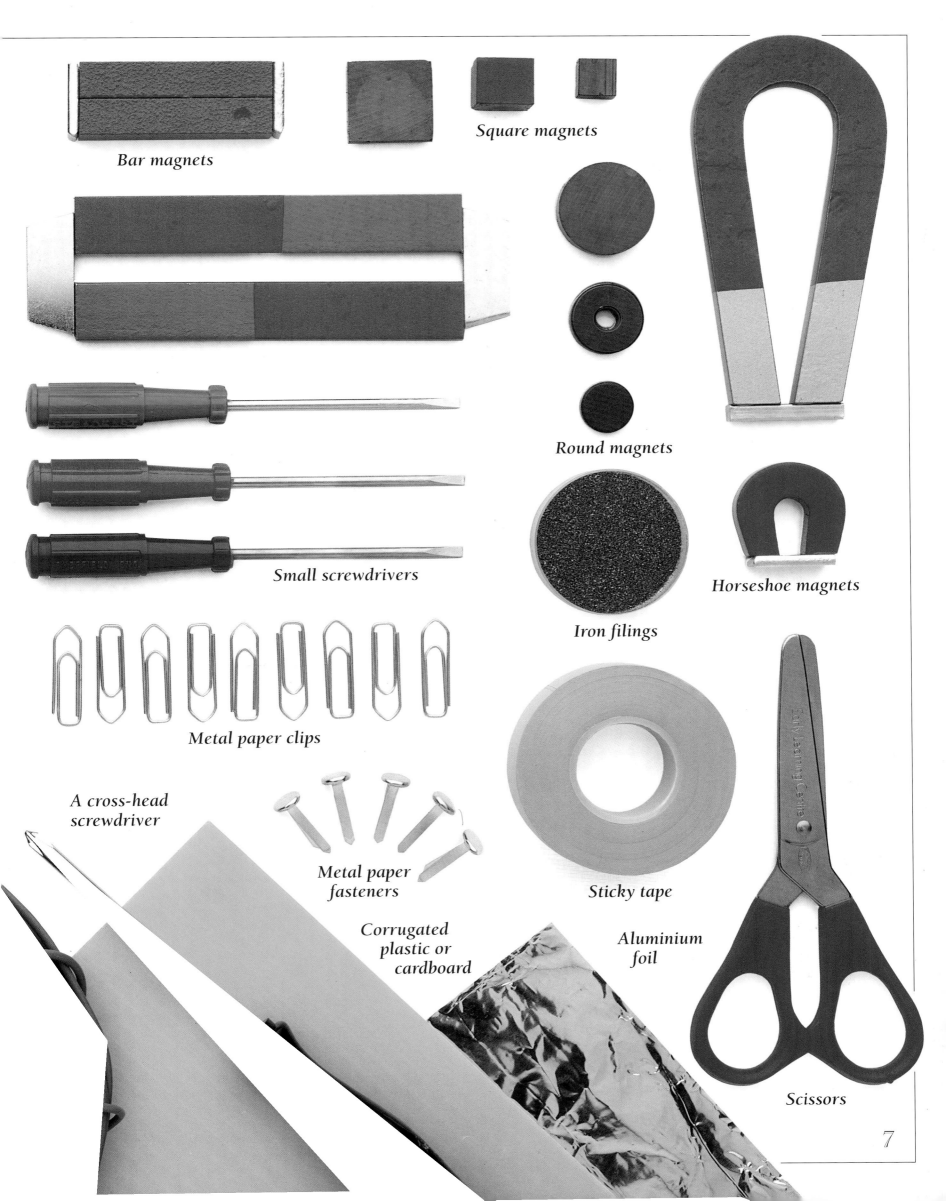

Bar magnets

Square magnets

Round magnets

Horseshoe magnets

Iron filings

Small screwdrivers

Metal paper clips

A cross-head screwdriver

Metal paper fasteners

Corrugated plastic or cardboard

Sticky tape

Aluminium foil

Scissors

BOTTLE VOLCANO

Have you ever noticed that the first few sips of a hot drink always seem much hotter than the rest of the drink at the bottom of the cup? This experiment shows you in a dramatic way exactly what happens when you mix hot liquids and cold liquids together. Remember to take care when using the glass containers.

You will need

String

A small bottle

A large glass jar

Red food colouring or ink

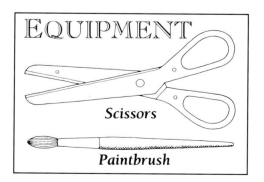

EQUIPMENT

Scissors

Paintbrush

Setting up the volcano

1 Cut a piece of string about 30 cm long. Tie one end of it firmly around the neck of the bottle, leaving the other end free.

2 Tie the other end of the string to the piece tied around the neck of the bottle, to make a loop of string for a handle.

3 Fill the large jar with cold water from a tap or jug. Don't fill it right to the top, as you need space to lower the bottle into it.

4 Ask an adult to fill the small bottle right up to the top with hot water. Stir in enough food colouring to turn the water red.

5 Hold the small bottle by the string handle and lower it gently into the jar of cold water, being careful to keep it level.

VOLCANO IN A JAR

As you lower the small bottle into the jar of cold water, the hot water shoots up into the cold water like a volcano. Soon all the hot water will rise to the top of the jar.

Why hot water rises

When water is heated, it expands (takes up more space). This makes the hot water lighter than cold water, so it rises to the surface of the cold water.

ON THE LEVEL

No two liquids are the same. Have you ever wondered why cream floats on top of milk, or why salad dressing separates into different layers? And did you know that some objects will sink in water but float on another liquid? Do this experiment and you can create a colourful giant cocktail and find out some fascinating things about different liquids at the same time.

You will need

Vegetable oil

Golden syrup

Things to float

Nuts

Plastic toys

Small metal objects

Small tomatoes

Water coloured with ink or food colouring

A large plastic container

Dried pasta

Grapes

What to do

1 Carefully pour golden syrup into the container over the back of the spoon, until the container is a quarter full.

2 Slowly pour the same amount of vegetable oil into the container. Then add the same amount again of coloured water.

3 Wait until the liquids have settled into layers. Then gently drop different objects into the container, to see what floats.

LIQUID COCKTAIL

The liquids separate into three layers, with the syrup on the bottom, the water above that and the oil on top of the water.
Liquids do this because some of them are lighter or less dense than others. A lighter liquid will float on top of a heavier or more dense liquid.

Floaters and sinkers

Some of the objects you drop into the container will sink. Others will float at different levels, depending on how heavy they are. Objects float best in dense liquids, as these support their weight best.

11

KITCHEN CHEMISTRY

You don't need special powders and test tubes to be a chemist. Everything around you is made of chemicals and you can do all kinds of interesting tests on things around the kitchen. Here and on the next three pages you can find out how to test things to see if they are acid or alkaline.

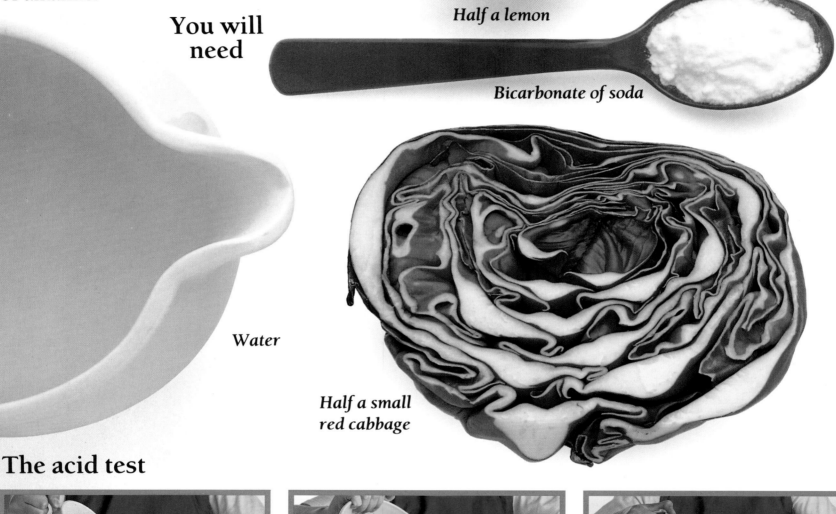

Blotting paper

Half a lemon

You will need

Bicarbonate of soda

Water

Half a small red cabbage

The acid test

1 Chop up the cabbage and put it in a bowl. Pour hot water over it and leave it to soak until the water turns purple.

2 Hold the sieve over the jug. Pour the cabbage water into the jug through the sieve, so that the cabbage stays in the sieve.

3 Pour a little purple cabbage water into several of the small jars. Label one jar *Control* and put it to one side.

12

Other things to test

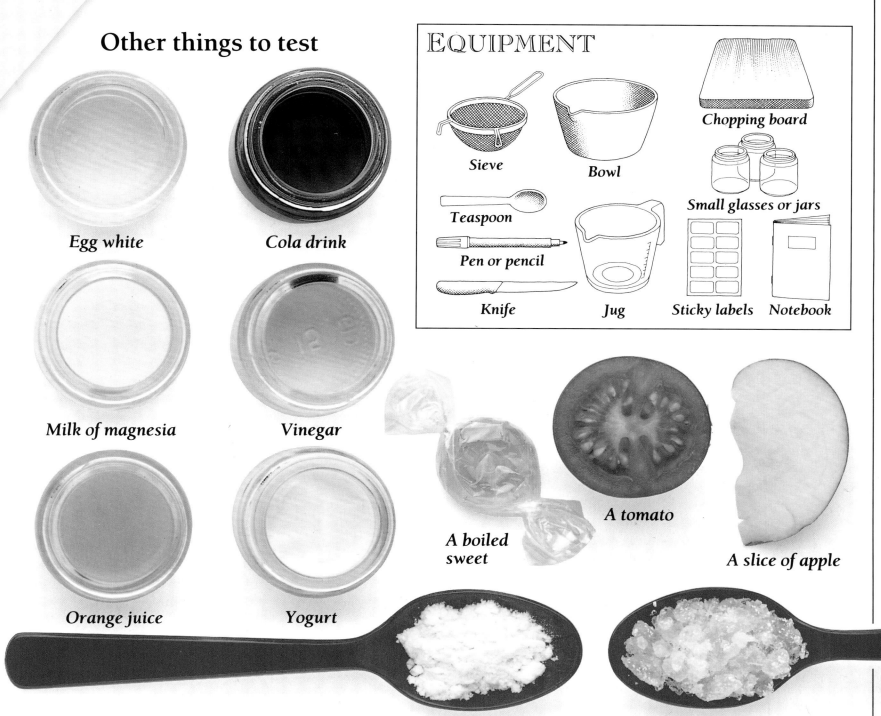

Egg white

Cola drink

EQUIPMENT

Sieve

Bowl

Chopping board

Teaspoon

Pen or pencil

Knife

Jug

Small glasses or jars

Sticky labels

Notebook

Milk of magnesia

Vinegar

A boiled sweet

A tomato

A slice of apple

Orange juice

Yogurt

Baking powder

Washing soda*

4 Pour a few drops of lemon juice into one of the other jars of purple cabbage water. Label the jar *Lemon juice*.

5 Mix a teaspoon of bicarbonate of soda with a little water. Stir it into a jar of purple water. Label it *Bicarbonate of soda*.

6 Do the same with all the other things you want to test. Label every jar to say what is in it as you do each test. Now turn the page.

Wash your hands after handling washing soda

13

MAGIC POTIONS

Changing colour

1 Squeeze a little lemon juice into two jars. Mix two teaspoons of bicarbonate of soda with water in a third jar.

2 Add some purple cabbage water to the two jars of lemon juice. The lemon juice should turn pink. Label one jar *Control*.

3 Add the bicarbonate of soda to the pink lemon juice, drop by drop. What happens to the colour of the lemon juice?

THE ACID TEST

Alkalis

If the cabbage water turns blue or green, as it does with bicarbonate of soda, the thing you have tested is an alkali.

Lemon

Bicarbonate of soda

Control jar
You keep the Control *jar to compare with the tests you do.*

Purple water with lemon juice added to it

Acids
If the purple cabbage water turns pink, as with the lemon juice, the thing you have tested is acid.

Purple water with a sweet added to it

Purple water with bicarbonate of soda added to it

The indicator paper test

1 Cut a piece of blotting paper into small strips about 1.5 cm wide. Cut a lot of strips so that you can test several liquids.

2 Dip the strips of blotting paper into purple cabbage water, then lay them on a saucer to dry. This might take a few hours.

3 Dip a strip of paper into each liquid you want to test. Try lemon juice, then bicarbonate of soda mixed with water.

CHANGING COLOUR

As you add the bicarbonate of soda (an alkali) to the lemon juice (an acid), the pink water turns purple. This shows that the liquid is no longer acid.

Lemon juice

Bicarbonate of soda

Purple water with lemon juice added to it

Pink water with bicarbonate of soda added to it

Strips of indicator paper

THE INDICATOR PAPER TEST
Scientists use indicator paper to test liquids to see if they are acid or alkaline. By dipping blotting paper into purple cabbage water, you have made your own indicator paper. When you dip indicator paper into an acid, it turns pink. When you dip it into an alkali, it turns blue or green.

15

SPOOKY SHADOWS

Make some scary puppets and entertain your friends to a spine-chilling shadow puppet theatre. Below are some puppet patterns to trace and opposite you can see how to make and operate the puppets.

Tracing paper

You will need

Thin card

Sticky tape

Thin sticks

A strong torch

EQUIPMENT

Scissors

Pencil

Puppet patterns

Vicious vampire

Terrifying tarantula

Scary spectre

Ghastly ghoul

Making the puppets

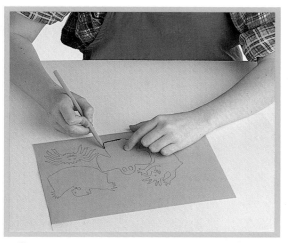

1 Trace the puppet patterns from the book on to tracing paper. (Or make up your own puppets and draw them on to card.)

2 Lay the tracing paper wrong side down on card. Scribble over the back of the lines you traced, to transfer them to the card.

3 Carefully cut the puppets out of the card. You can use a pencil to make holes for eyes. Tape each puppet to the end of a stick.

SHADOW THEATRE

You need two people to set up the theatre: one to hold the torch and the other to work the puppets. Make sure the room is dark, then shine the torch at the wall and move the puppets around between the torch and the wall. With practice, you can make the shadows grow bigger and even change shape.

Monster shadows

Light rays are straight. So the closer a puppet is to the torch, the more light it blocks and the bigger the shadow.

VANISHING COLOURS

Light looks white, but it is really made of rainbow colours. Make this simple multi-coloured wheel and you will be able to make colours disappear, then appear again, as if by magic. Where do the colours go and why? Spin the wheel, then read about what happens at the bottom of the page opposite.

You will need

Thin card

A short, sharp pencil

A glue stick

Tracing paper

Coloured paper (red, orange, yellow, green, blue and purple)

Making the colour wheel

EQUIPMENT

Sharp pencil

Scissors

Pair of compasses

Ruler

1 Open the compasses to 5 cm and draw a circle on the card. Then mark six points, 5 cm apart, around the circle with the compasses.

2 Join each pair of opposite points together, so the three lines cross in the centre of the circle. Cut out the circle.

3 Trace a segment of the circle. Glue it on to card and cut it out. Draw round the shape on each colour of paper and cut it out.

4 Glue the pieces of coloured paper to the circle of card in this order: red, orange, yellow, green, blue and purple.

5 Punch a hole in the centre of the circle with the tip of the scissors. Push the pencil through the hole, as shown.

SPINNING COLOURS

Spin the colour wheel fast and watch what happens. Which colour or colours can you see? When the wheel spins fast, your eyes and brain working together cannot see each colour separately, so the colours blur together to make a different colour.

As the colour wheel slows down, the blurring lessens, and your eyes and brain can pick out the different colours again. Try making other wheels in just two or three colours. Do you always see the same colour when you spin them?

19

SPLITTING COLOURS

Many of the inks and dyes that are used to colour things are really mixtures of several different coloured chemicals or *pigments*. The two experiments here show you how to separate the different coloured pigments in felt-tip pens and the food colouring used in sweets.

You will need

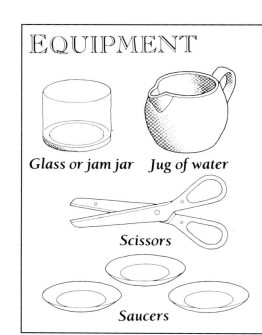

EQUIPMENT

Glass or jam jar   Jug of water

Scissors

Saucers

Coloured felt-tip pens

White blotting paper

Half a teaspoon of salt

Coloured chocolate sweets

Felt-tip pen test

1 Cut out a rectangle of blotting paper big enough to roll into a tube that you can slide into the glass you are going to use.

2 Make blobs of different colours* about 4 cm from the bottom of the blotting paper with the felt-tip pens.

3 Pour a little water into the glass and stir in the salt. Roll the blotting paper into a tube and stand it in the glass.

Dark colours are the most interesting colours to test.

20

Sweet test

1 Choose three colours to test. Put five or six sweets the same colour in each saucer. Add a few drops of water to them.

2 Turn the sweets over and stir them round a little, so that most of the colour runs off them and colours the water.

3 Cut three strips of blotting paper. Lay a strip into each of the saucers as shown, with one end in the coloured water.

FELT-TIP PEN TEST

As the water rises up the blotting paper, it dissolves the pigments in the ink blots and carries them up with it. The different pigments move up the paper at different speeds, so they separate and you can see bands of different colours.

SWEET TEST

The pigments used on the sweets are absorbed by the blotting paper in the same way as the pigments in the felt-tip pens. As they move up the blotting paper, they separate. Some of the colours only contain one pigment.

FINGERPRINT KIT

No two people have the same fingerprints. This makes them valuable clues when detectives are investigating a crime. Fingerprints are usually invisible, but detectives use scientific methods to reveal fingerprints found at the scene of a crime and compare them with suspects' fingerprints. Read what to do below and you can do some detective work of your own.

You will need

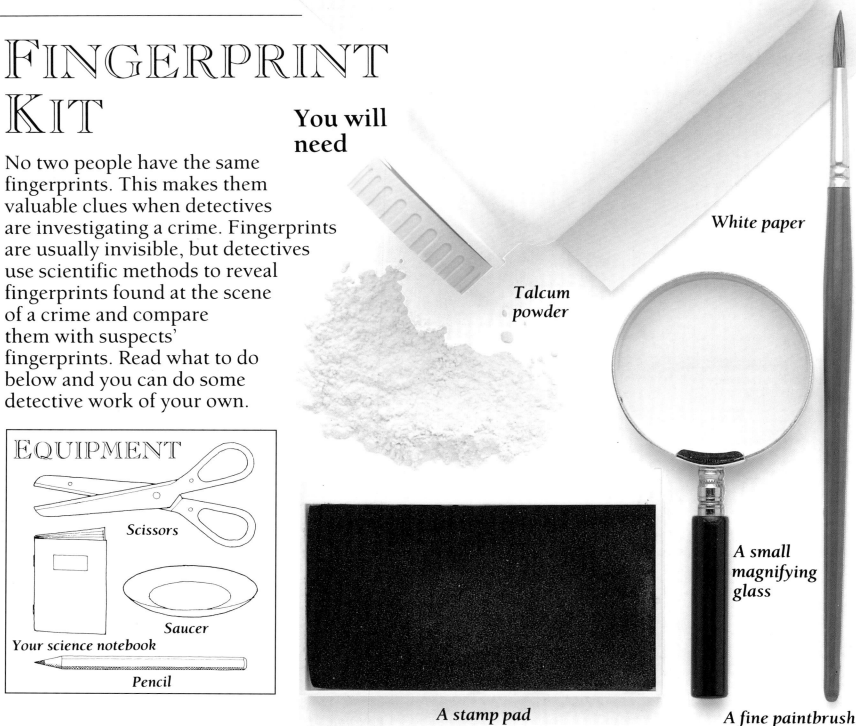

White paper

Talcum powder

A small magnifying glass

A stamp pad

A fine paintbrush

EQUIPMENT

Scissors

Saucer

Your science notebook

Pencil

Taking fingerprints

1 Press the pad of one of the suspect's fingers lightly on the stamp pad. Roll it from side to side, to cover it with ink.

2 Press the suspect's finger firmly on a piece of paper. Hold it as shown in the picture and roll it from side to side.

3 Take prints of all the suspect's fingers and label them. Then examine them carefully. Are all the prints the same?

Dusting for fingerprints

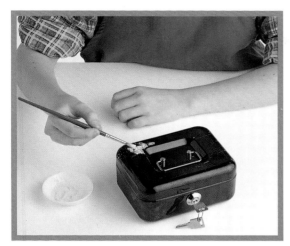

1 Pour some talcum powder into a saucer. Dust the talcum powder lightly on something hard and shiny that people often touch*.

2 Blow gently on the places that you have powdered. Most of the powder will blow away, except where there are greasy marks.

3 Now brush the powdered spots very lightly with a fine paintbrush. Any fingerprints will gradually appear, as if by magic.

FINGERPRINT FILE

When you have taken all the suspects' fingerprints, cut them out and glue them into your science notebook. Then you can compare them with any fingerprints you find around your home.

Use a magnifying glass to study the details of fingerprints.

Suspect's fingerprint

Fingerprint found on cash box

* The edges of windows, door knobs and light switches are good places to try.

MAKING MUSIC

Why do things make noises? There are noises all around you all of the time, but you cannot see them. Try making your own musical instruments though and you will not only have lots of fun, but will also learn a lot about how sounds are made at the same time. Here you can find out how to make a harp from elastic bands, a xylophone from bottles and pan pipes from drinking straws. Turn the page to see the finished instruments, then start twanging, banging and blowing!

A glue stick

You will need

8 plastic drinking straws

A metal spoon

Food colouring or ink

Water

Several glass bottles the same size

Making the pan pipes

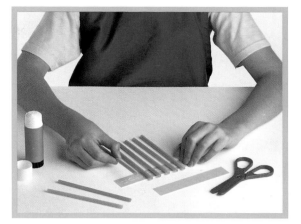

1 Spread glue along one strip of card. Glue the eight straws to the card at equal distances, with the tops of the straws in line.

2 Glue the second strip of card over the top of the straws. Trim the straws so that each one is shorter than the one before.

Making the harp

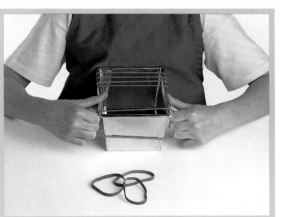

1 Stretch eight elastic bands around the baking tin or plastic box as shown, so that they are all the same distance apart.

2 To give the elastic bands different notes, tighten each one by pulling it and catching it on the edge of the tin.

Making the xylophone

1 Stand the bottles in a row. Pour water into them, so that each bottle contains a little more water than the one before.

2 To make the xylophone look prettier, add a few drops of food colouring to each bottle of water and stir it in.

---

*2 strips of card
14 cm by 2.5 cm*

EQUIPMENT

Scissors

Jug

Paintbrush

Thick elastic bands

A baking tin or plastic box

YOUR OWN BAND

Now that you have made your musical instruments, see if you can play a tune on any of them. The instruments shown here are plucked, blown and banged upon, but each of them really makes sounds in the same way. All sounds, both nice and nasty, are carried by the air around you. When you play a musical instrument, it makes the air around it vibrate. The air carries this vibration to your ears. Your eardrums vibrate and you hear the sound made by the instrument.

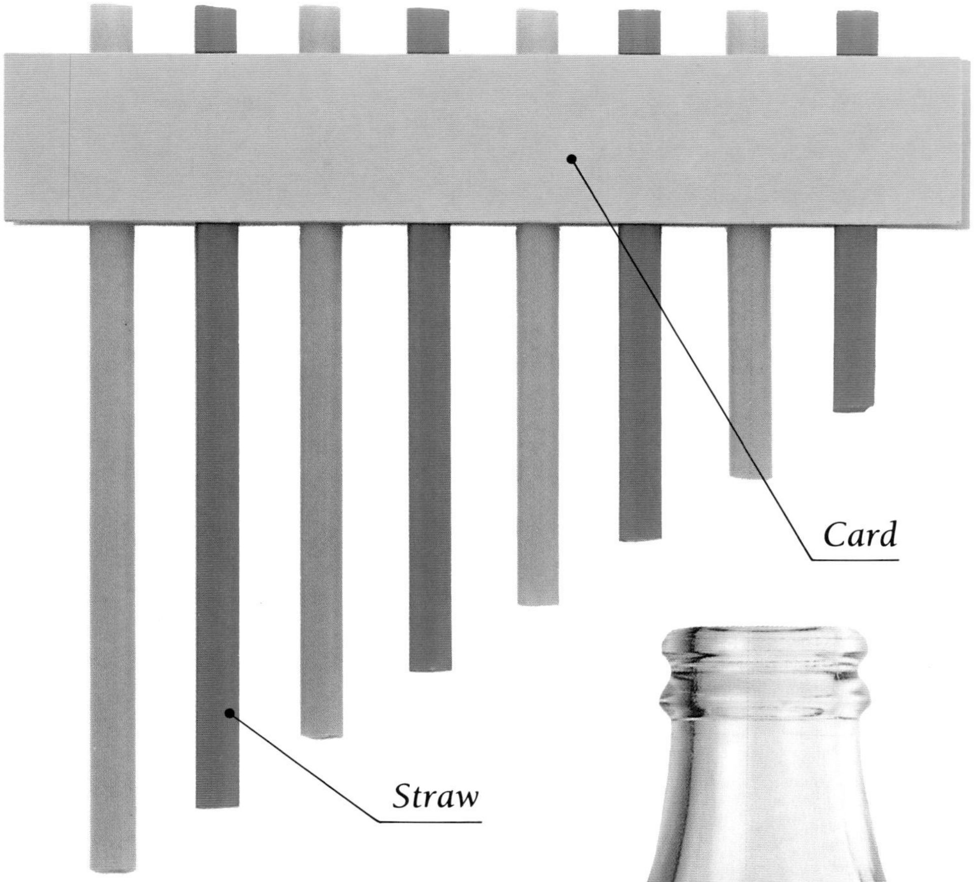

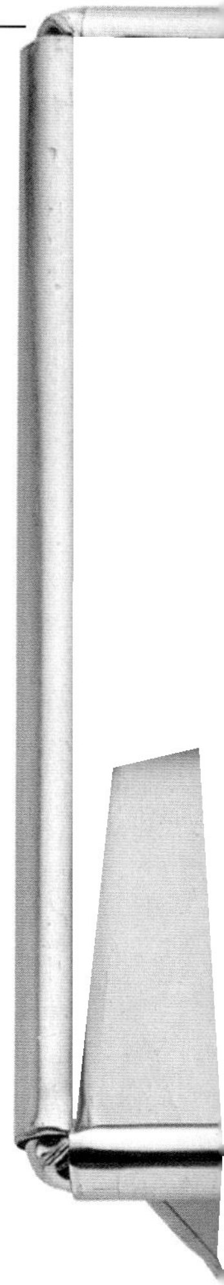

PAN PIPES

The pipes are a simple wind instrument. Hold them to your mouth with the straws pointing downwards, as shown here, and blow across the tops of the straws. You will hear quiet, flute-like sounds. The shorter the straws are, the higher the notes they make.

Card

Straw

BOTTLE XYLOPHONE

The xylophone forms the percussion part of your band. Tap each bottle in turn with the spoon to hear what note it makes. The more water there is in the bottle, the lower the note it produces.

If you adjust the amount of water in the bottles, you should find that you can play part of a musical scale by striking each bottle in turn.

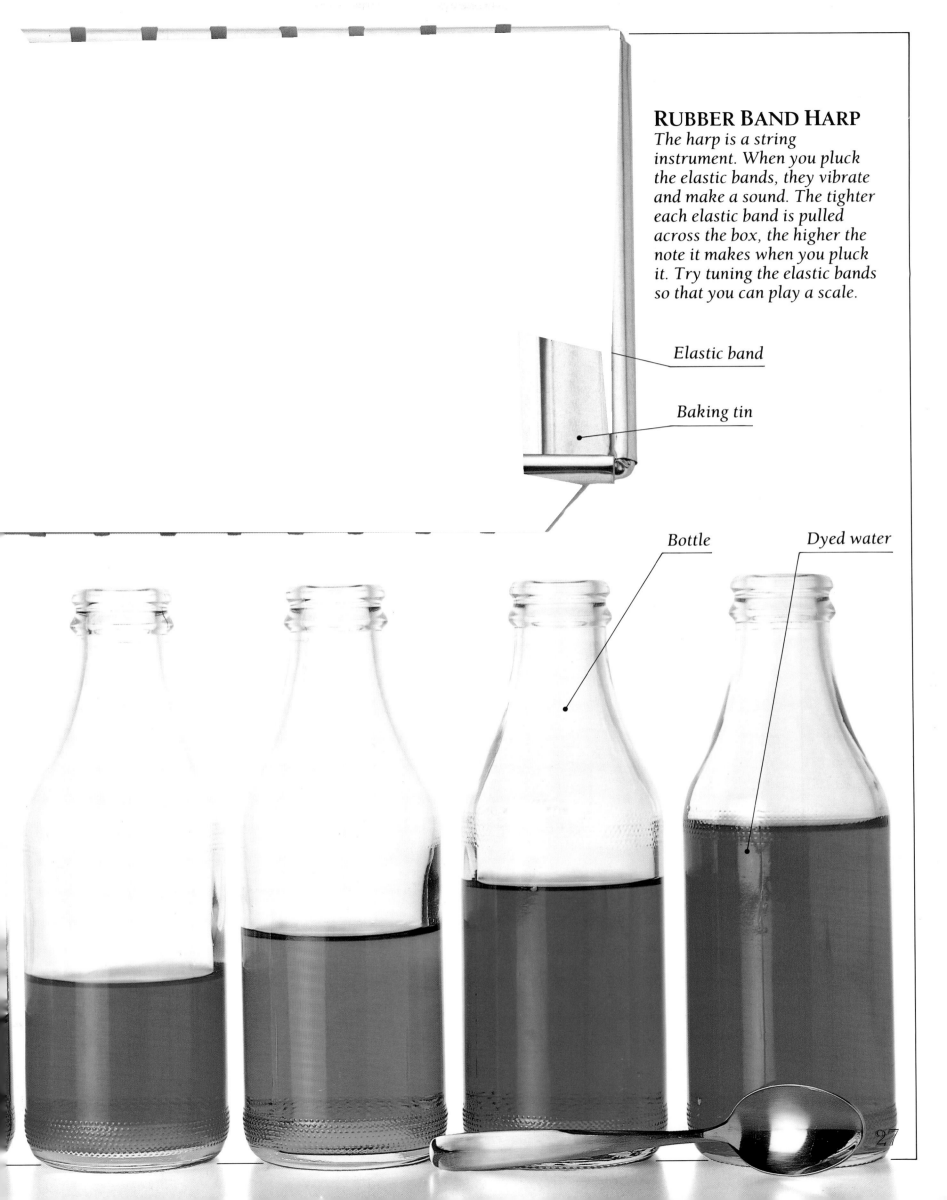

RUBBER BAND HARP

The harp is a string instrument. When you pluck the elastic bands, they vibrate and make a sound. The tighter each elastic band is pulled across the box, the higher the note it makes when you pluck it. Try tuning the elastic bands so that you can play a scale.

Elastic band

Baking tin

Bottle

Dyed water

27

MULTI-COLOURED FLOWERS

Why do we put flowers in a vase of water and where does the water in the vase go? In this clever experiment you use food colouring or ink to reveal something that you would normally never see: how flowers drink and where the water goes.

You will need

Jug of water

Different coloured inks or food dyes

White carnations

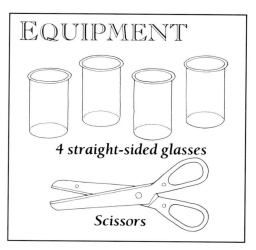

EQUIPMENT

4 straight-sided glasses

Scissors

What to do

1 Pour about 2 cm of different-coloured food colouring or ink into each glass. Add about 2 cm of water to each glass.

2 Trim the flower stems to 5 cm taller than the glasses. Cut along the stems of two flowers, to split them in half lengthwise.

3 Stand a flower in each glass of water. Stand each half of the two split-stemmed flowers in different coloured water.

Red flower

Blue flower

Pink flower

Green flower

Tiny veins

Look closely at the flowers and you will see the tiny veins that carry water to each part of the flower petals. They have been stained by the food colouring.

Colour change

Leave the flowers in a warm room for a few hours and they will slowly turn the same colour as the water in which they are standing.

Pink and blue flower

Red and green flower

Two-tone flowers

Each half of the flowers with the split stems will turn the same colour as the water in which that half of the stem is standing. This shows that the tiny tubes for water in each part of the flower stem lead to a specific part of the flower.

29

WEATHER STATION

Set up your own weather station and you will be able to keep a record of your local weather. Here and overleaf you can find out how to make a rain gauge, for measuring rainfall, a barometer, to show changes in the air pressure and a wind vane, so that you know which way the wind is blowing.

You will need

Food colouring or ink

Waterproof sticky tape

A glue stick

A short pencil with an eraser on the end
Three long pencils

A drinking straw

A shallow bowl

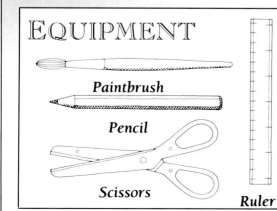

EQUIPMENT

Paintbrush

Pencil

Scissors

Ruler

A yogurt pot

A large, straight sided plastic bottle

Materials

Thin card

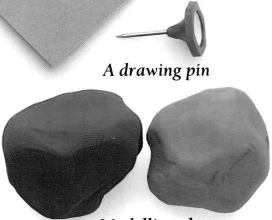

A drawing pin

Modelling clay

A narrow, clear plastic bottle*

* Use the narrowest bottle you can find.

Making the wind vane

1 Make a hole in the centre of the base of the yogurt pot. Push the short pencil into it, so the eraser end sticks out as shown.

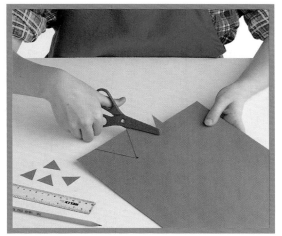

2 Cut four small triangles out of thin card. Then cut out a triangle about 3 cm deep and a bigger one about 5 cm deep.

3 Glue the four small triangles to the base of the yogurt pot, so that they point in four different directions, as shown.

4 Cut 1 cm slits at both sides of each end of the straw. Slot the two big triangles into them, pointing in the same direction.

5 Push the drawing pin through the centre of the straw**. Then stick the pin into the eraser. Make sure the vane can spin easily.

6 Make a sausage of modelling clay and bend it into a ring. Push the clay around the base of the wind vane.

** Ask an adult to help you.

31

Weather Watch

Making the rain gauge

1 Cut off the top quarter of the large plastic bottle, using the scissors. Ask an adult to help you make the first cut.

2 Slide the top of the bottle upside down into the base of the bottle, to act as a funnel. Tape the edges together, as shown.

3 Cut tiny strips of sticky tape. Tape them to the side of the bottle about a centimetre apart, to act as a measuring scale.

Making the barometer

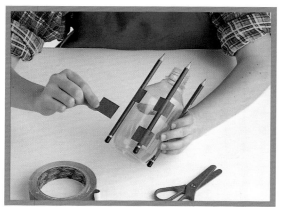

1 Tape three long pencils to the small plastic bottle. The points of the pencils should stick out above the top of the bottle.

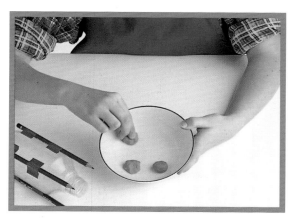

2 Using the bottle to help you, stick three lumps of modelling clay to the bottom of the bowl, for the pencils to go into.

3 Half fill both the bowl and the bottle with water. Add a few drops of food colouring or ink to the water with the paintbrush.

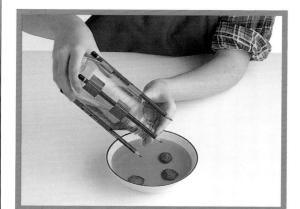

4 Cover the top of the bottle with your hand. Turn it upside down and lower it under the water in the bowl.

5 Take your hand away from the mouth of the bottle. Keeping the bottle straight, push the pencils firmly into the modelling clay.

6 Cut tiny strips of sticky tape. Tape them to the side of the bottle to make a scale, as when making the rain gauge.

32

RECORDING THE WEATHER

Stand your wind vane and rain gauge outside. Keep the barometer indoors, away from direct sunlight. Check your weather station every day and make a record of any changes in your science notebook. As well as reading the instruments you have made, write down how many hours of rain or sun there have been and note what sort of clouds are in the sky.

How the barometer works

A barometer measures air pressure. Air presses down on the water in the bowl. When the air pressure rises, the air pushes down harder on the water, making the water in the bottle rise higher up the scale. When the air pressure drops, the water level in the bottle drops lower.

The water level in this barometer is also slightly affected by changes in air temperature.

If your rain gauge has a plastic base, fill the base with water before putting the rain gauge outside.

Measuring the rainfall

When it rains, check every day how far up the scale the water comes. Make a note of the reading, then empty the rain gauge.

Which way is the wind blowing?

Stand the wind vane outside on a flat surface. Use a compass to position it so that one of the triangles points north. Mark the triangles north, south, east and west. Write down which direction the wind is blowing from. The north wind, for example, blows from north to south.

FLYING PAPER

How do aeroplanes fly? Launch a piece of paper into the air and it will just swoop down to the ground. But if you make a plane with the piece of paper, it will fly really well.

Here and on the next three pages you can find out how to make an amazing superglider and helicopter. They are not only fun to make and play with, but will also teach you a lot about how things fly.

You will need

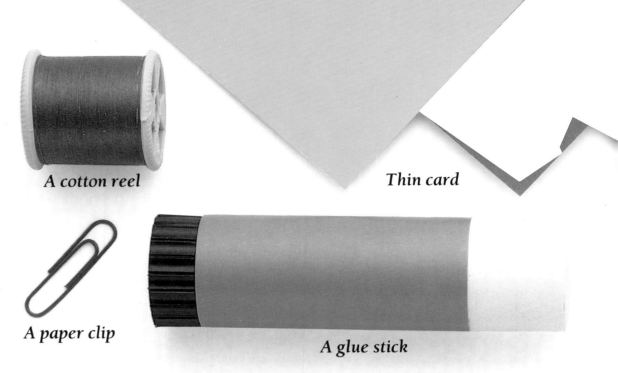

A cotton reel

Thin card

A paper clip

A glue stick

A drinking straw 13 cm long

Tracing paper

A small lump of modelling clay

String

EQUIPMENT

Scissors

Ruler *Pencil*

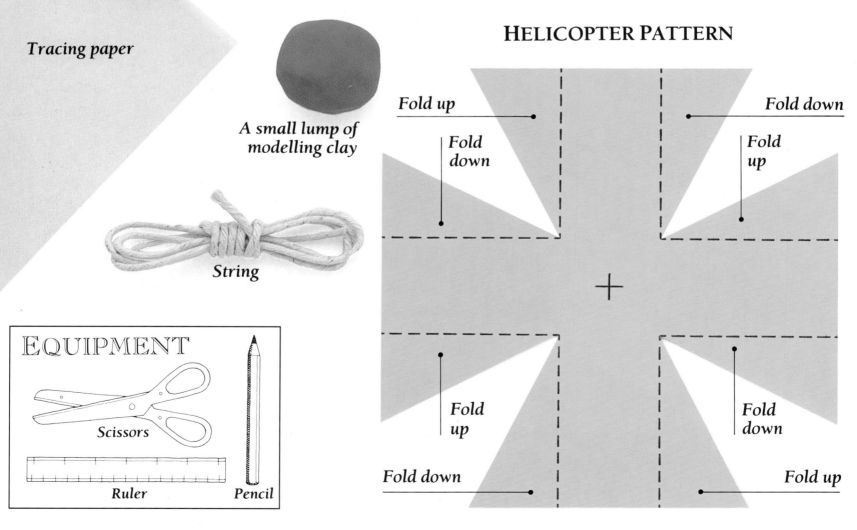

HELICOPTER PATTERN

Fold up   *Fold down*

Fold down   *Fold up*

+

Fold up   *Fold down*

Fold down   *Fold up*

SUPERGLIDER PATTERN

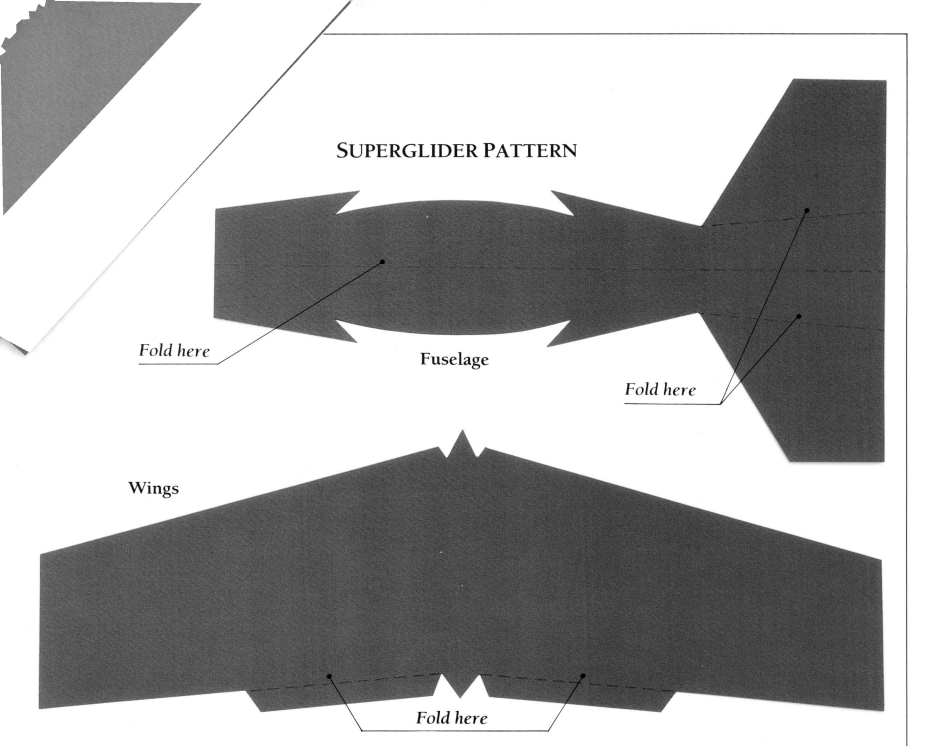

Fold here

Fuselage

Fold here

Wings

Fold here

Making the superglider

1 Trace the outlines of the two superglider pattern pieces onto tracing paper. Trace along the fold lines using dotted lines.

2 Turn the tracing paper over. Lay it on the card and scribble over the lines you have traced, to transfer the pattern to the card.

3 Cut the wings and fuselage out of the card. Score along the fold lines, using your ruler and the point of your scissors *.

* This helps to make the folds sharper.

Now turn the page.

FLYING HIGH

Superglider (continued)

4 Fold the fuselage in half along the fold line, then open it out again. Fold down the two tail fins and the two wing flaps.

5 Slot the back of the wings into the back notches on the fuselage. Slot the front of the wings into the front two notches.

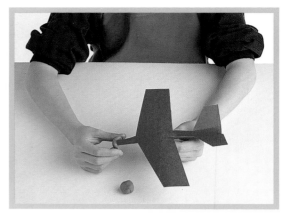

6 Put the paper clip on the nose of the aeroplane. Fold a piece of modelling clay around the paper clip, to act as a weight.

Making the helicopter

1 Trace the pattern for the helicopter rotor on to tracing paper. Trace the fold lines, using dotted lines.

2 Turn the tracing paper over. Lay it on the card and scribble over the lines you have traced, to transfer the pattern to the card.

3 Cut the helicopter rotor out of the card. Score along the fold lines, using your ruler and the point of your scissors.

4 Each rotor blade has two fold lines. Fold one side of each rotor blade up and the other side down, along the fold lines.

5 Make a hole in the middle of the rotor. Spread glue around one end of the straw. Push the straw through the hole in the rotor.

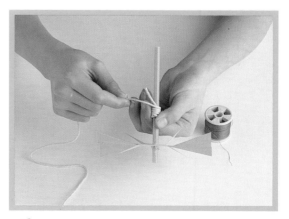

6 Make a loop in one end of the string. Wind string anti-clockwise over the loop around the straw beneath the rotor.

Helicopter launch

Push the straw into the cotton reel. Hold the cotton reel in one hand and pull the string hard with the other.

As the helicopter rotors spin, they push air down, squashing the air under the rotors. The pressure of this air pushes the helicopter into the air.

Taking off

To launch the superglider, hold it just behind the nose and let it go gently. The plane flies because the shape of the wings makes the air flow faster over the wings than below them. The pressure of air below the wing is greater than it is above the wing, helping to keep the plane airborne for longer.

If the superglider keeps tipping upwards and then diving, try adding a little more modelling clay to the nose. If the glider dives too fast, the nose may be too heavy, so remove some modelling clay.

MAGIC MAGNETS

Magnets have special powers that seem to be magic. Their power is called magnetism, and it can move certain objects around without even touching them. Below you can find out more about magnets, then on the next few pages use their powers in some fun projects.

A selection of different magnets

You will need

Snake pattern

A variety of small household objects and steel paper clips

Cotton thread

6   7   8   9   10   11   12

17   16   15   14   13   12   11   10   9   8   7   6   5   4   3   2   1   0

A ruler

Pieces of coloured felt

Glue

Sticky tape

Magnetic attraction

EQUIPMENT

Scissors   *Felt pen*

Hold a magnet close to each of the objects you have collected. Which objects does the magnet pick up? What are they made of?

Making the snake

1 Trace the snake pattern on the opposite page, then cut it out in felt. Decorate your snake with small pieces of coloured felt.

2 Give the snake felt eyes and a tongue. Tie a short piece of thread to a paper clip. Slide the paper clip on to the snake's head.

3 Tape a magnet to one end of the ruler. Tape the thread from the snake to the table. Try making a kite or flower as well.

It's magnetic magic!

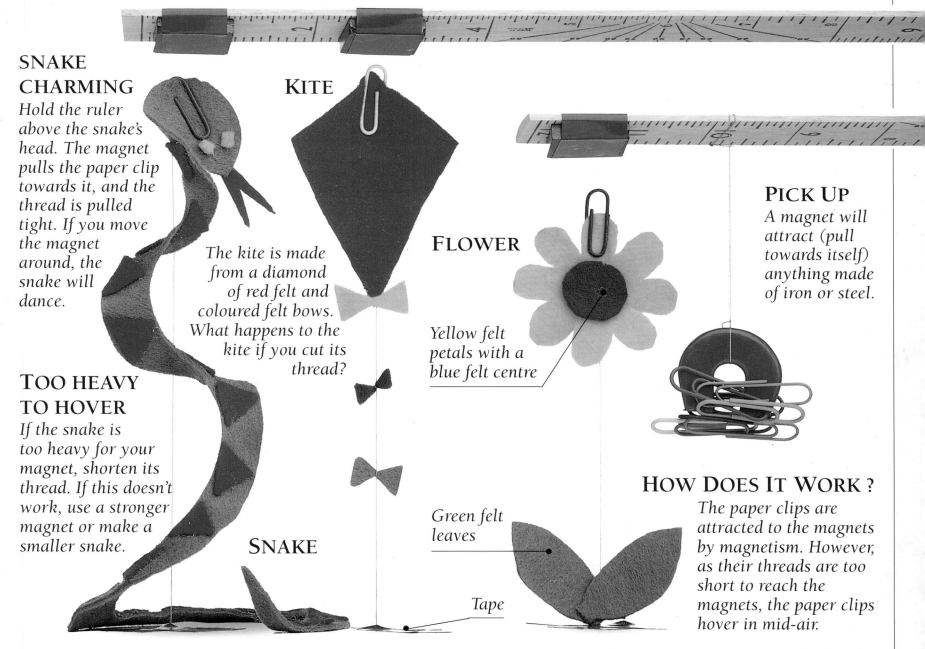

SNAKE CHARMING

Hold the ruler above the snake's head. The magnet pulls the paper clip towards it, and the thread is pulled tight. If you move the magnet around, the snake will dance.

KITE

The kite is made from a diamond of red felt and coloured felt bows. What happens to the kite if you cut its thread?

TOO HEAVY TO HOVER

If the snake is too heavy for your magnet, shorten its thread. If this doesn't work, use a stronger magnet or make a smaller snake.

SNAKE

FLOWER

Yellow felt petals with a blue felt centre

Green felt leaves

Tape

PICK UP

A magnet will attract (pull towards itself) anything made of iron or steel.

HOW DOES IT WORK ?

The paper clips are attracted to the magnets by magnetism. However, as their threads are too short to reach the magnets, the paper clips hover in mid-air.

39

FRIDGE MAGNETS

Brighten up your kitchen with colourful decorations that cling to the fridge! Fridge magnets can come in all shapes and sizes and they are very easy to make. The magnets stick to the outside of the fridge, because it is made of steel. Try sticking them to other metal things around your home.

EQUIPMENT

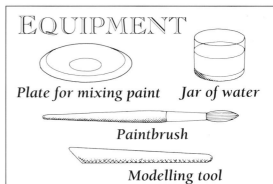

Plate for mixing paint   *Jar of water*

Paintbrush

Modelling tool

You will need

Coloured oven-hardening clay*

Clear nail varnish

Poster paints

Glue

Plain self-hardening clay

Small, flat magnets

What to do

1 Model any shape you like out of clay. Harden your shapes by following the instructions on the clay packet very carefully.

2 Paint the shapes made of plain clay and leave them to dry. Brush all of your shapes with clear nail varnish.

3 When the varnish is dry, glue a magnet to the back of each shape. Once the glue has set, the fridge magnets are ready to use.

*Ask an adult to help you to harden shapes made from this clay.

Magnetic fridge friends

The whale and the monster were made from coloured oven-hardening clays and the acrobats, fish, and dinosaur from plain, self-hardening clay, which was painted.

The fridge magnets are attracted to any object made of iron or steel.

WALLY

MAGNETIC MINNOWS

MONSTER ATTRACTION

DINOSAUR ON DUTY

Make an army of your favourite dinosaurs to guard the fridge!

ACROBATIC ADVENTURE

Arrange your acrobats in incredible balancing positions.

PAPER CLIP PALS

A magnet's amazing powers will even attract things made of steel or iron through card and felt. Here you can find out how to use magnetism to make a crazy, dancing clown, and a useful hedgehog that will keep your paper clips tidy.

You will need

Coloured felt pens

Three bar magnets

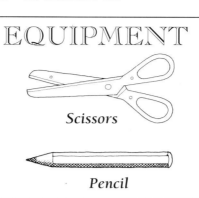

EQUIPMENT

Scissors

Pencil

Lots of steel paper clips

Coloured felt

A glue stick

A paper fastener

White card

Making the clown

1 Cut out the shape of a clown's body, like this one, and colour it in. Draw a circus scene on a larger piece of card.

3 Push a paper fastener through the clown's body, then through the middle of the circus scene. Fold back the legs of the fastener.

Making the hedgehog

1 Wrap a rectangle of felt round a magnet. Glue it down. Cut out a semi-circle for the head, and shapes for the feet, nose and eyes.

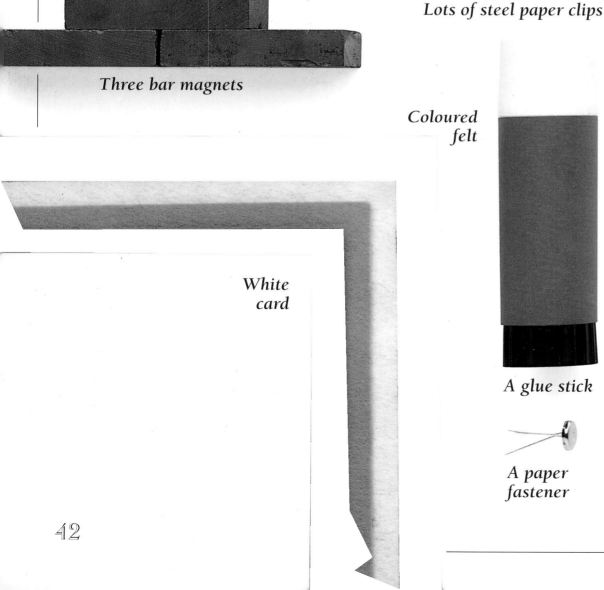

DANCING CLOWN

2 Cut out hands and feet for the clown, and colour them in. Join each one to the body with a chain of three linked paper clips.

4 Move one magnet around behind the circus scene. What happens to the clown's arms and legs as you do this?

Paper fast

The clown's paper clip arms and legs are attracted to the magnet as it moves around behind the card.

With practice, you can make your clown do some amazing dance steps!

HOGGING THE PAPER CLIPS

2 Glue the semi-circle into a cone and stick it to the body. Glue the feet, nose, and eyes in place. Then add the paper clips.

Steel paper clips

Plastic-covered paper clips for the hedgehog's spikes

Blue and white felt eyes

Black felt triangle for the nose

Black felt feet

MAGNETIC FISHING

Set up this unusual fishing game and compete with your friends to see who has the mightiest magnet and can catch the most fish in the shortest time. You need a magnet for each player*, so the more magnets you have, the more people can play the game.

You will need

A magnet for each person playing

Lots of paper clips

Sticky tape

A small stick for each player

A large bowl of water

String

Aluminium foil

Setting up the game

1 Fold the aluminium foil in half, then in half again. Cut fishes out of the folded foil, using the first fish as a pattern piece.

2 Slide a paper clip onto the front end of each aluminium foil fish. Drop all the fish into the bowl of water.

3 Cut pieces of string about 20 cm long. Tie a magnet to one end of each piece. Tie the other end to a stick and tape it down.

How to play

Catch the fish by picking them up with the magnets. If two players catch the same fish, they must put it back in the bowl. The player who catches the most fish is the winner.

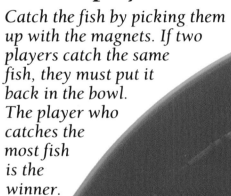

MAGNETIC FIELDS

A magnet's invisible powers are contained within its 'magnetic field'. You can see the pattern of a magnetic field by putting iron filings near a magnet. Iron filings usually leap towards a magnet, but if you put them in sticky syrup, they will form magnetic patterns very slowly. Stir up the filings in the syrup, every time you use the mixture.

EQUIPMENT

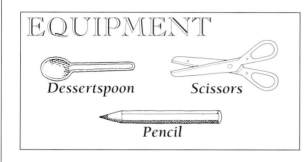

Dessertspoon   *Scissors*

Pencil

You will need

A selection of different magnets

Some string

Iron filings

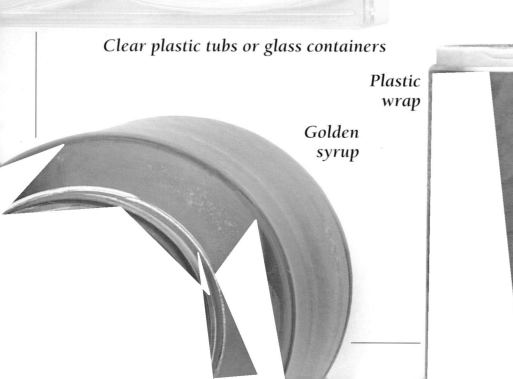

Clear plastic tubs or glass containers

Plastic wrap

Golden syrup

Making the mixture

Sprinkle a dessertspoonful of iron filings into the syrup. Stir gently until the iron filings are evenly mixed into the syrup.

Magnetic patterns

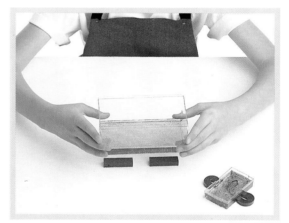

Pour some mixture into each tub. Place magnets underneath or at the sides of the tubs, then watch as the magnetic fields appear.

3-D fields

Fill a glass with mixture. Cover a bar magnet in plastic wrap, and tie it to a pencil with string. Hang the magnet in the middle of the glass.

Fields of filings

Each magnet forms a magnetic field pattern. Test magnets of different shapes, sizes and strengths, and compare the fields they make. Then look at the fields you can produce when you put two or more magnets near each other. Here are some of the patterns we found.

MAGNETIC PATTERNS

When a magnet is placed near the mixture, the iron filings become magnetised. The filings line up in the field of the magnet, and slide very slowly towards the ends of the magnets, where the magnetism is strongest. When two magnets are near each other, their field patterns change shape.

Plastic container

The magnetic fields around these strong bar magnets go through the sides of the container.

SLOW MOTION

Iron filings move slowly through the syrup and cluster around the ends of the magnets.

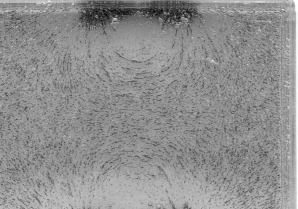

Horseshoe magnet

Pencil

String

3-D FIELDS

Turn the glass around to see the field surrounding the magnet, as it hangs in the middle of the mixture.

Keep your magnet clean by covering it in plastic wrap before you lower it into the syrup.

47

POLES APART

Every magnet has a north pole and a south pole, like the Earth. These poles are the two opposite ends, or sides, of a magnet, where its powers are strongest. You can find out more about magnetic poles, how to identify them and why magnets behave oddly when they are together, in the experiments below. Opposite you can see how to make your own magnets, as well as an amazing turtle compass that really works.

Poster paint

A bottle top

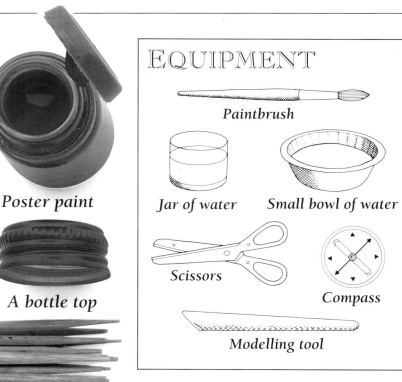

EQUIPMENT

Paintbrush

Jar of water   *Small bowl of water*

Scissors

Compass

Modelling tool

Wooden skewers

A horseshoe magnet

You will need

A steel needle

Coloured modelling clay

Strong bar magnets

Ring magnets

North or south pole?

Hang a bar magnet above the compass, as shown*. When it stops moving, the end pointing north is the magnet's north pole.

Pole position

Try pushing the north poles, then the south poles of two magnets together. What happens? Next, try a north and a south pole together.

Making the lion

Paint some skewers, cut them in half, and stick them in some clay around a bar magnet. Model a clay lion. Sit it on another bar magnet.

Making the clown

Stick three skewers into some clay. Put some ring magnets onto the skewers. Model a clown from clay, and stick it on the top magnet.

48

* The magnet will affect the compass needle if it is too close.

Turtle compass

Float the turtle in a bowl of water.

1 Stroke a needle, 30 times from its point to its eye, with the south pole of a magnet. Make a light, flat turtle from clay.

2 Push the turtle onto the open end of the bottle top. Stick the needle point firmly into the turtle's tail, directly opposite its head.

BOUNCING CLOWN

The clown bounces on the invisible magnetic fields of the magnets.

The clown's body is hollow so that it is light enough to bounce on the magnets.

TURTLE COMPASS

The needle becomes a magnet when it is stroked by a magnet. As it floats in the bowl, it is affected by the Earth's magnetic field. The turtle's head points to the North and the eye of the needle in its tail points South.

OPPOSITES ATTRACT...

The north pole of one magnet and the south pole of another magnet attract (pull towards) each other, and the magnets snap together.

Modelling clay clown

Modelling clay lion

South pole

South pole

Skewer cage bars

The top magnet will not float if the lion is too heavy.

North pole

North pole

...LIKE POLES REPEL

Two north poles or two south poles together, repel (push away from) each other, so the magnets 'float' one above the other.

Modelling clay base

LEVITATING LION

Put the magnet with the lion in the cage, with like poles sitting on top of each other. The magnets repel each other, making the top magnet float. Try turning the top magnet, or removing the cage bars.

49

MAGIC BALLOONS

Some of the most interesting science experiments help you to see the effects of invisible forces at work around you. Strange things can happen to the most ordinary everyday objects. Here you can find out how to give balloons powers that seem magical.

A sheet of paper torn into small pieces

You will need

Balloons

Sugar

What to do

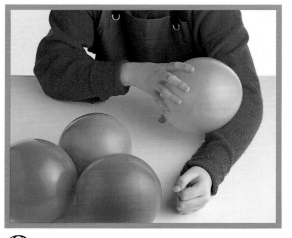

1 Blow up the balloons. You may need an adult to help you do this. Tie the end of each balloon into a firm knot.

2 Now rub each balloon hard against your sweater. The tricks work best if the sweater you are wearing is made of wool.

3 Hold one balloon just above the torn up pieces of paper. What happens? Then try holding a balloon just above some sugar.

"MAGICAL" ATTRACTION

The balloons pick up the torn up paper and sugar, as if by magic.

Electrical charges

Rubbing a balloon against wool charges it with static electricity. Static electricity is made up of electrical charges which can move small things without even touching them! The sugar and paper are pulled on to the surface of the balloon by the charges.

Everything contains electrical charges. You cannot see them, but you can rub them off some things and on to others, making static electricity. This type of electricity doesn't flow like the electricity in an electrical circuit.

51

MAKING CONNECTIONS

Batteries can really make things happen! They produce electricity, which can turn a motor or light a bulb. Before the electricity can flow, it must have a path from one side, or terminal, of the battery to the other. This path is called a circuit. On this page you will find out how to connect a battery in a circuit, to light a bulb. You can also make a switch to turn the bulb on and off.

You will need

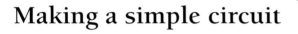

Wire

A 4.5V battery

A 3.5V or 4.5V bulb

A bulb holder

Paper fasteners   *A steel paper clip*

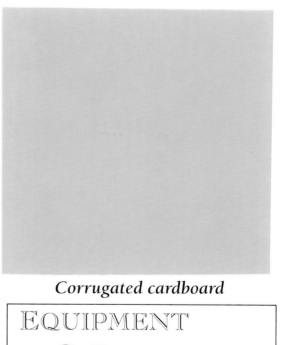

Corrugated cardboard

Making a simple circuit

1 Cut two pieces of wire, and carefully strip about 2 cm of plastic from their ends. Twist the bare metal strands together.

2 Twist a wire tightly around each of the battery terminals, as shown. Make sure that the bare wire is touching the terminal.

3 Touch one wire to the bottom of the bulb and one to the side. You have made a complete circuit, and the bulb will light up.

4 Screw the bulb into the bulb holder, and attach the wires as shown, using a small screwdriver. The bulb still lights up.

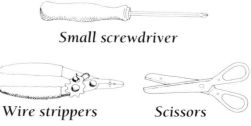

EQUIPMENT

Small screwdriver

Wire strippers   *Scissors*

52

Making a switch

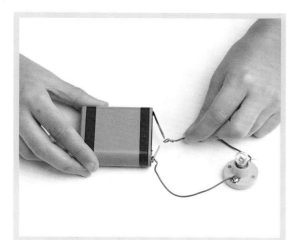

5 Take one of the wires off the battery. The bulb will go out, because there is no longer a complete circuit.

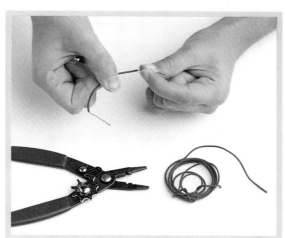

6 Cut another piece of wire. Strip away 2 cm of plastic from each end of the wire and twist the metal strands, as before.

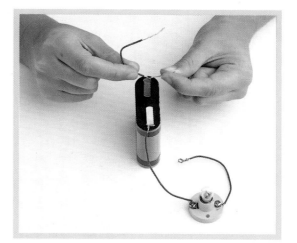

7 Attach one end of the wire to the disconnected terminal of the battery. The other end of the wire will connect to the switch.

8 Carefully cut out a rectangle of cardboard, about 3 cm by 5 cm. This is the base that will hold the pieces you need for the switch.

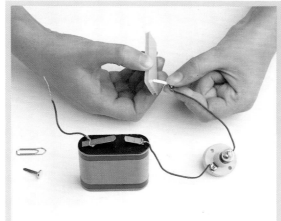

9 Wind the end of the wire from the bulb holder firmly around a paper fastener and push the fastener through the cardboard.

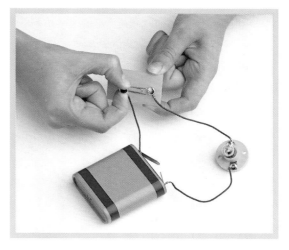

10 Do the same with the end of the other wire, as shown, but this time put a paper clip around the paper fastener as well.

THE COMPLETED CIRCUIT

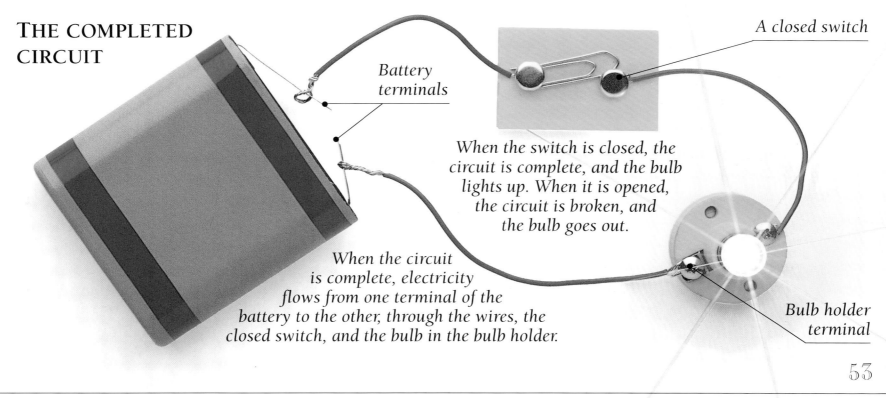

A closed switch

Battery terminals

When the switch is closed, the circuit is complete, and the bulb lights up. When it is opened, the circuit is broken, and the bulb goes out.

When the circuit is complete, electricity flows from one terminal of the battery to the other, through the wires, the closed switch, and the bulb in the bulb holder.

Bulb holder terminal

HAUNTED HOUSE

With a little imagination, you can transform an old cardboard box and three simple bulb circuits into an eerie, haunted house, full of ghosts that glow in the dark and giant spiders with hairy legs. Find out how to wire up the circuits and decorate the box below. Then, turn the page to see the finished house as the clock strikes midnight, and the haunting begins!

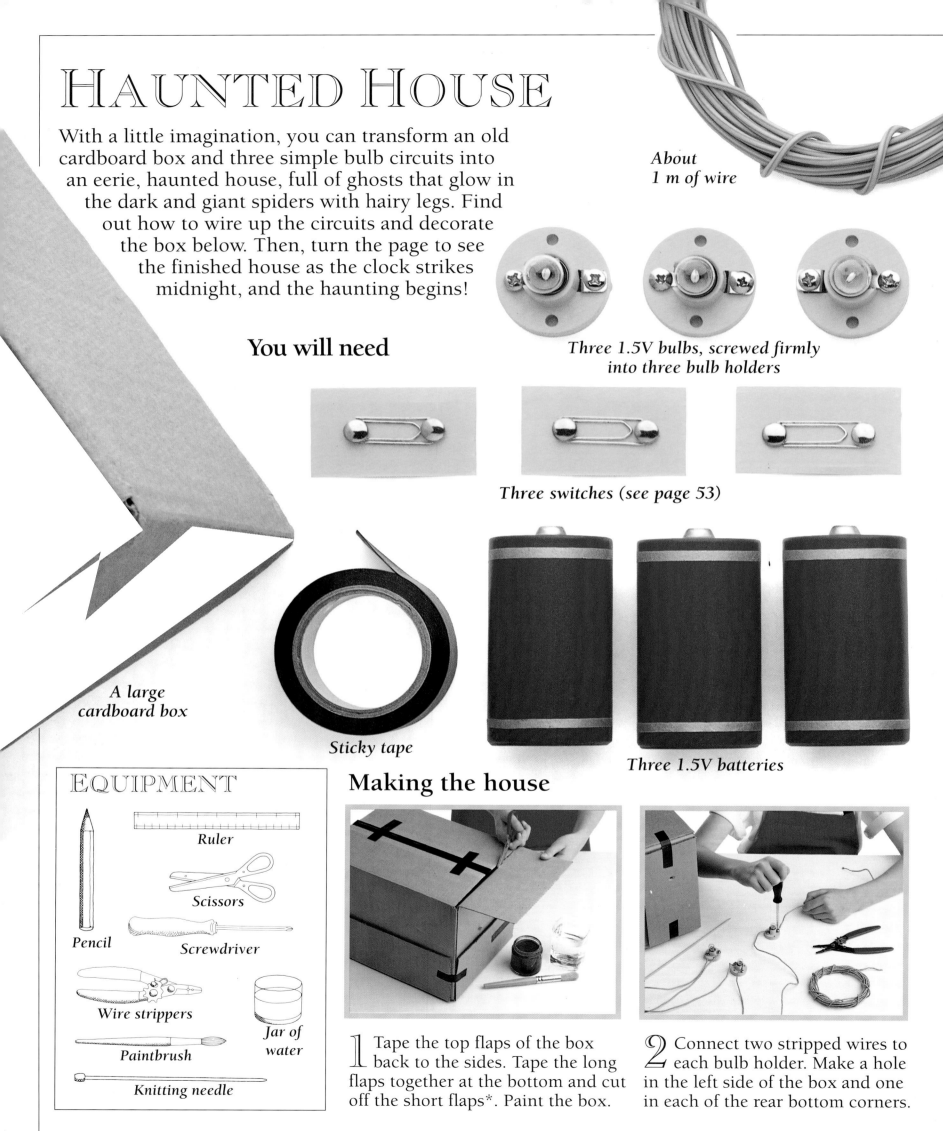

About 1 m of wire

Three 1.5V bulbs, screwed firmly into three bulb holders

You will need

Three switches (see page 53)

A large cardboard box

Sticky tape

Three 1.5V batteries

EQUIPMENT

- *Ruler*
- *Scissors*
- *Pencil*
- *Screwdriver*
- *Wire strippers*
- *Jar of water*
- *Paintbrush*
- *Knitting needle*

Making the house

1 Tape the top flaps of the box back to the sides. Tape the long flaps together at the bottom and cut off the short flaps*. Paint the box.

2 Connect two stripped wires to each bulb holder. Make a hole in the left side of the box and one in each of the rear bottom corners.

54

*Save one short flap for the fireplace in step 5.

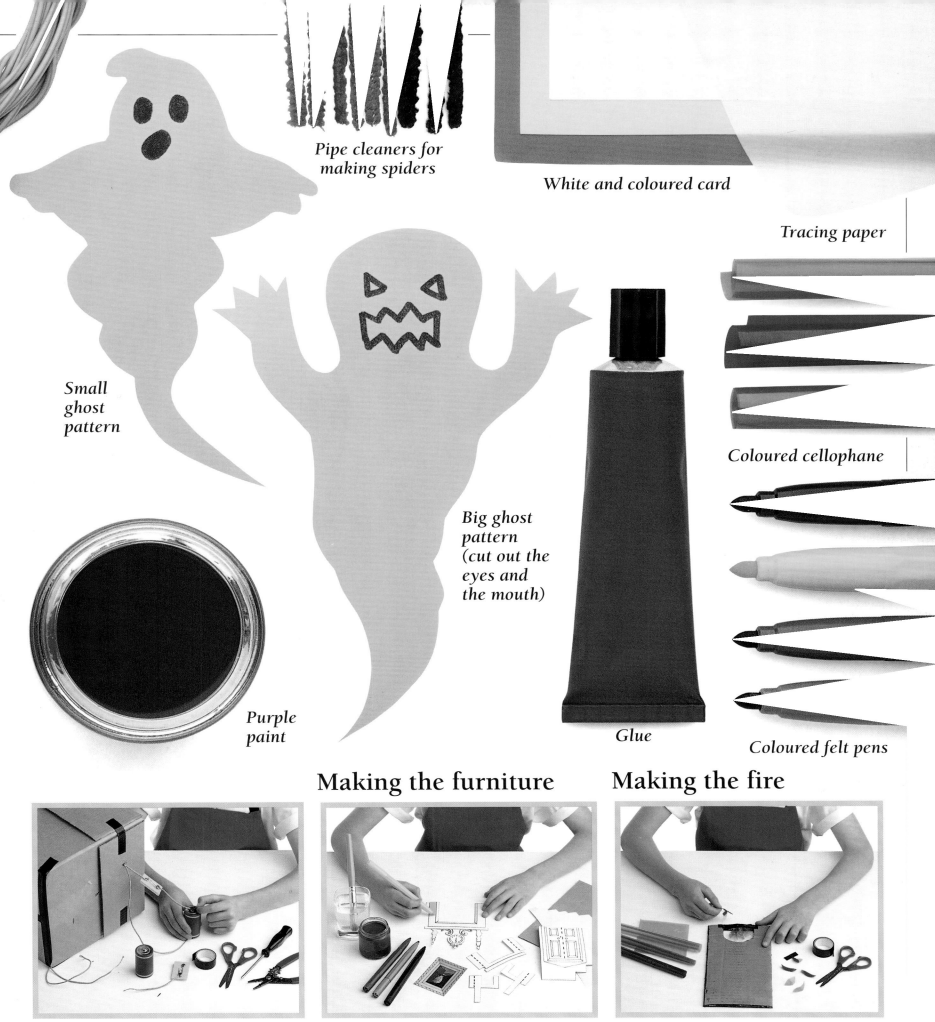

Pipe cleaners for
making spiders

White and coloured card

Tracing paper

Small
ghost
pattern

Big ghost
pattern
(cut out the
eyes and
the mouth)

Coloured cellophane

Purple
paint

Glue

Coloured felt pens

Making the furniture

Making the fire

3 Thread the wires from one bulb
holder out through each hole.
Connect a switch and a battery to
each pair of wires, in a circuit.

4 Draw a fireplace, a portrait, two
chairs, a table, and a staircase
with a door in it, on white card.
Cut them out and colour them in.

5 Paint the spare box flap. Cut a
small arch out of it. Cut out
flame shapes from the cellophane.
Tape them to the back of the arch.

GHOSTS ON GUARD

Moving in

Tape the fireplace in front of the bulb in the left corner, and the staircase in front of the bulb in the right. Glue the furniture in place.

Making the spiders

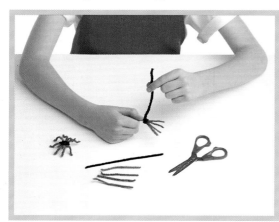

Cut two brown pipe cleaners in half. Wind a black pipe cleaner round the middle of the four halves, as shown. Bend the legs.

Making the ghosts

Trace the ghost patterns from page 55 onto coloured card and cut them out. Draw eyes and a mouth on the two small ghosts.

The finished haunted house

As the clock on the mantelpiece strikes midnight, the ghosts start to prowl...

GLOWING GHOUL

Glue the bulb holder to the wall of the box, then stick the big ghost in front of it, so that the bulb is totally hidden. The ghost glows spookily when the bulb is lit.

Glue the switch for each circuit to the sides of the box. Close the switches to make the bulbs light up.

The wires are connected to the top and bottom of the battery with tape.

SMALL SPOOKS

Stick the small ghosts to the wall with glue, or suspend them from the ceiling with dark threads.

The cellophane flames glow like a real fire when the bulb behind the fireplace is alight.

A FAMILY PORTRAIT
You could glue a small photograph of yourself to the wall instead of drawing a portrait.

TERRIFYING TARANTULAS
Glue the spiders to the box, and bend their legs so they look as though they are scuttling about.

IN FULL GLOOM
The walls, ceiling, and floor are painted a deep purple to make the room look dark and creepy.

CREEPY CUPBOARD
Stick a small ghost to the back of one door, as though it is escaping from the cupboard under the stairs.

This switch controls the bulb hidden behind the cupboard doors.

Tape the table and chairs firmly to the floor of the box with dark tape.

Open the cupboard doors under the stairs to let an eerie light shine through.

57

STOCK CARS

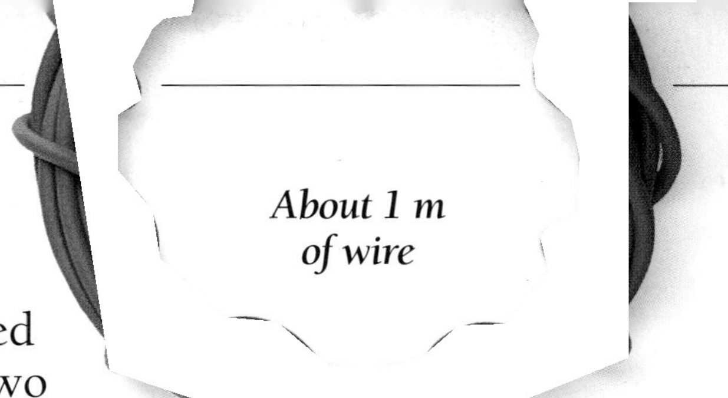

Did you know that a car's lights are powered by a battery? The lights are connected in two different types of circuit. Headlights are connected 'in series' (the bulbs are wired together, one after the other, in a circuit). The indicators are connected 'in parallel' (two separate circuits are connected to the same battery). Here you can find out how to make a 'smashing' stock car with working headlights and indicators.

About 1 m of wire

Four wooden skewers

You will need

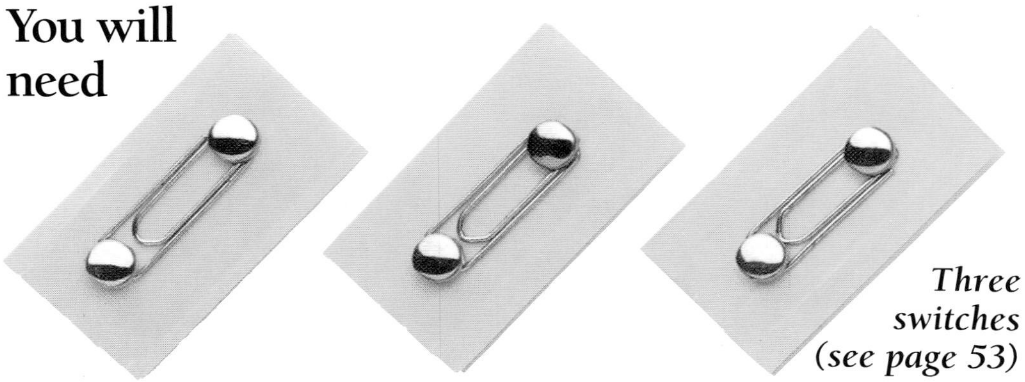

Three switches (see page 53)

Glue

Three 1.5V batteries

An egg box

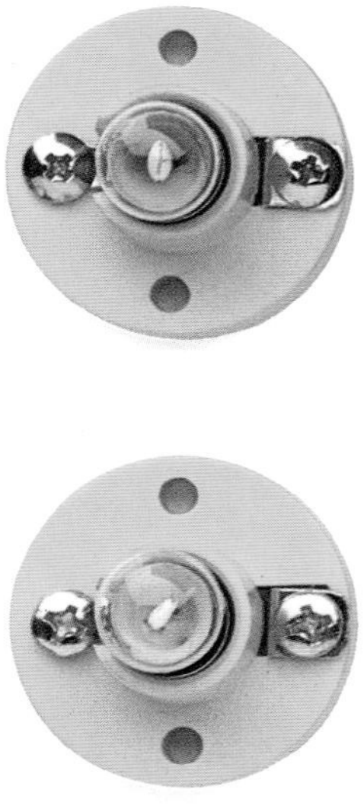

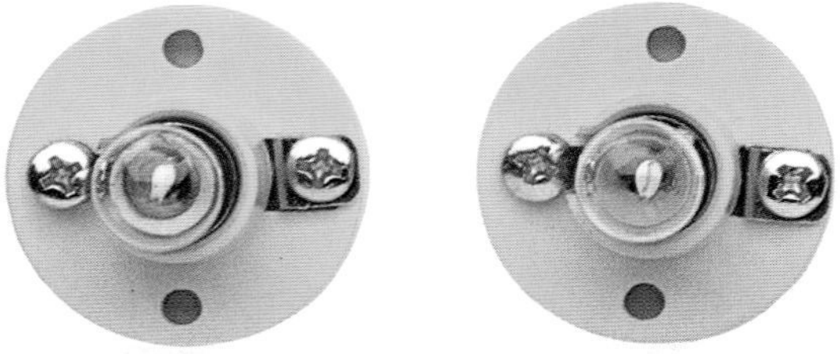

Four 1.5V bulbs in bulb holders

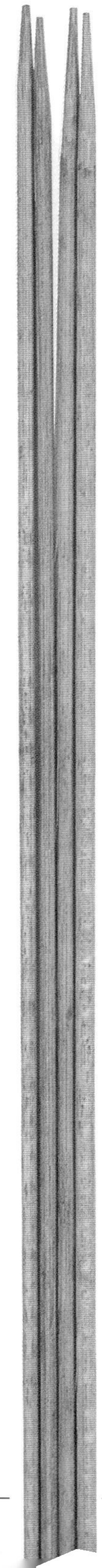

EQUIPMENT

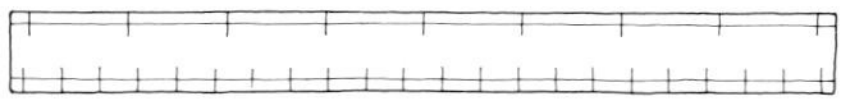

Ruler

Pencil

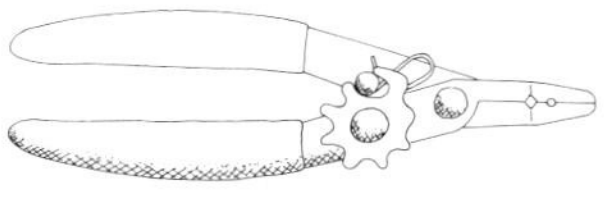

Wire strippers

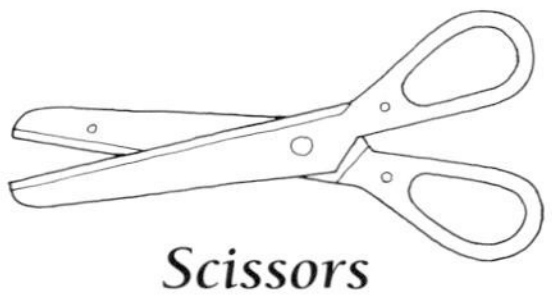

Scissors

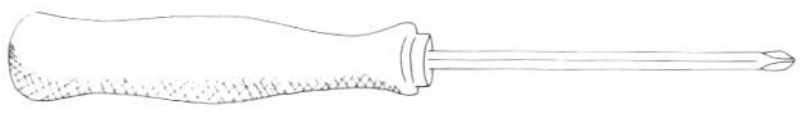

Cross-head screwdriver

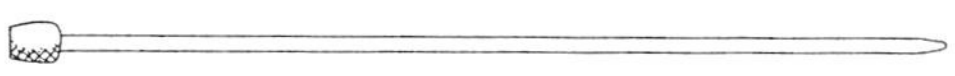

Knitting needle

58

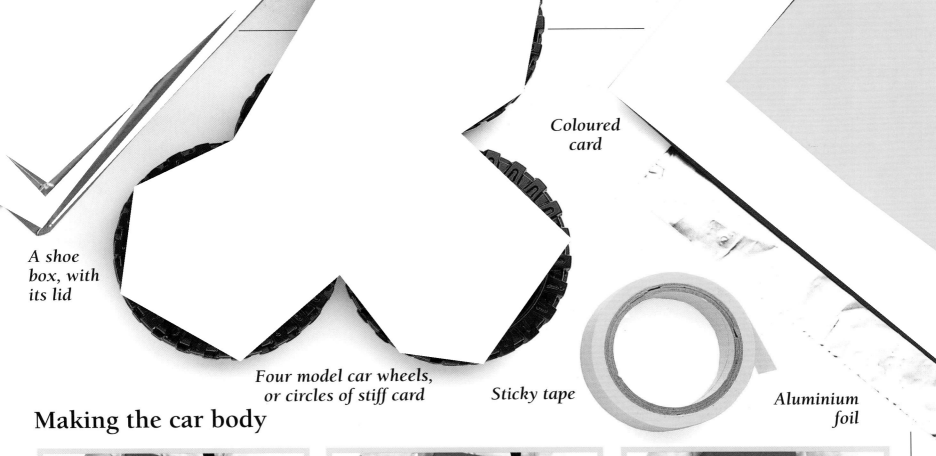

A shoe box, with its lid

Coloured card

Four model car wheels, or circles of stiff card

Sticky tape

Aluminium foil

Making the car body

1 Cut away the box, as shown, making sure that the long sides of the car are the same*. Tape the back flap to the sides of the car.

2 Cut down the box lid to fit the top of the car and a windscreen. Fold down the cut end to make the windscreen, and tape it in place**.

3 Push a wheel on to each pair of skewers. Make holes for axles: two holes at the rear of the car and two below the windscreen*.

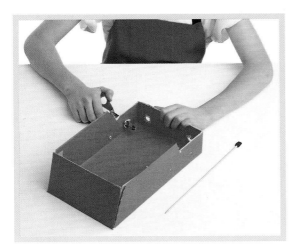

4 Make two holes, large enough for a bulb to go through, in the front of the car*. Then, make a hole on either side of the bonnet*.

5 Poke the skewers through the axle holes and push wheels on to the ends. Decorate the stock car with pieces of coloured paper

6 Cover two cups from an egg box with foil. Make a big hole in the bottom of each*, then glue one over each headlight hole.

*Ask an adult to help you with this.

**The piece of lid left over becomes the car's bonnet.

LIGHTING-UP TIME

Headlights 'in series'

Indicators 'in parallel'

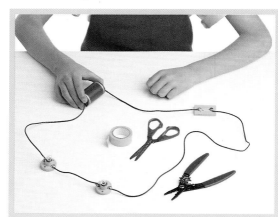

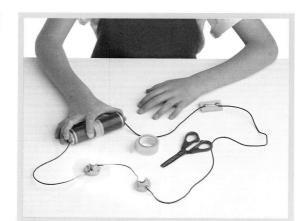

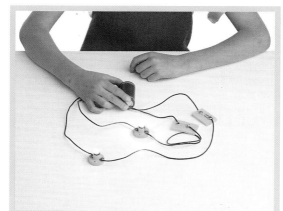

1 Connect two bulbs 'in series' in a circuit, as shown. The lights are dim as one battery is too weak to power two bulbs wired in series.

2 Tape the top of one battery to the bottom of another, in series. Connect the batteries to the circuit, as shown. Now the lights are bright.

3 Connect two separate circuits, each with a bulb and a switch, to one battery, as shown. Bulbs wired in parallel shine brightly.

Stock car smash-up

The car headlights are wired in series because both lights need to be on at the same time. Indicators are used one at a time, so they are wired in parallel, with separate switches.

Glue a large paper number to the roof, sides and bonnet of your stock car.

BRIGHT LIGHTS!

Foil cups around the headlights reflect the light forward from the bulbs. This makes the headlights appear brighter.

Fitting the lights

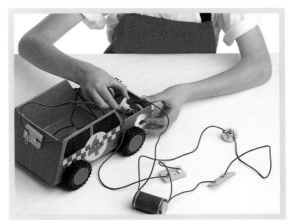

1 Put the headlights circuit into the car. Glue the switch to the back of the car. Push one bulb through each foil cup, as shown.

2 Glue a foil-covered card circle over both side holes. Make a big hole in each, as before. Push an indicator bulb through each hole.

3 Put the circuit in the car. Glue the left indicator switch to the left side of the car and the right indicator switch to the right side.

Black paper windscreen and windows

GO-FASTER STRIPES
Glue small squares of yellow paper on to strips of red paper.

The bonnet and roof lids hide the batteries and wires inside.

LEFT TURN
The foil disc around the indicators reflects the light from the bulb so that the indicator can be seen.

HUB CAPS
Circles of coloured card hide the skewer axles.

61

BUG PROBES

Electricity can flow through some materials but not others. It can't flow through plastic, so you must strip the plastic from the ends of a wire to make a connection. Materials that let electricity flow through them are called conductors. Make a battery bug probe, then look for conductors around your home.

Two 1.5V batteries

A 4.5V battery

EQUIPMENT

Scissors

Sticky tape

Glue stick

Wire strippers

Screwdriver

Aluminium foil

You will need

Some sequins

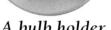

Three pipe cleaners

A bulb holder

A 3.5V bulb

Two 2.5V bulbs

Flex or wire

Some coloured card and paper

Making the leggy bug

1 Put a square of foil between the top of one 1.5V battery and the bottom of the other, as shown. Tape the batteries firmly together.

3 Screw the 3.5V bulb into the holder. Connect the 12 cm and 8 cm wires to the holder. Tape the 8 cm wire to the top of the battery.

Making the smiley bug

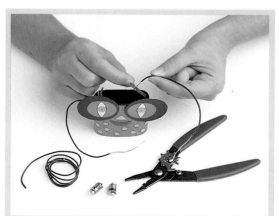

1 Decorate the 4.5V battery with coloured paper. Cut two wires and strip their ends. Attach a wire to each of the battery terminals.

Leggy bug

Decorate the body of the bug with tiny circles of coloured paper and card.

Tape pipe cleaner legs to the underside of the bug.

Coloured sequins glued on to two ovals of card

Wire antennae with aluminium foil balls at the stripped ends

Aluminium foil is a good conductor of electricity.

2 Cut a 25 cm, a 12 cm, and an 8 cm length of wire and strip their ends. Connect the 25 cm wire to the bottom of the battery.

4 Tape the holder to the batteries. Wrap them in paper with the two free wires sticking out at the top. Push foil balls on to the wires.

2 Wind each wire round a screwdriver, to make it curly. Twist the end of each wire firmly around a 2.5V bulb, as shown.

BUG CONDUCTORS

Touch the bulbs of the smiley bug, or the foil balls of the leggy bug, to different materials around your home. The bulbs will light up, if the material conducts electricity.

Smiley bug

Touch the bottoms of the bulbs to the object being tested.

Coloured paper and sequin eyes

WHAT HAPPENS

When you touch the bug's antennae together, or to a material that conducts electricity, the bulb lights up because the circuit is complete. When you touch them to a material that doesn't conduct electricity, the circuit is broken and the light goes out.

ROBOT MASK

Make a robot mask that glows in the dark! Its special coloured lamps, called LEDs (Light Emitting Diodes), only light up one way round, so always connect the shorter leg of the LED to the negative ⊖ terminal of the battery and the longer leg to the positive ⊕ terminal. Make sure that the wires from the LEDs are long enough to let you hide the switch and batteries in your pocket.

You will need

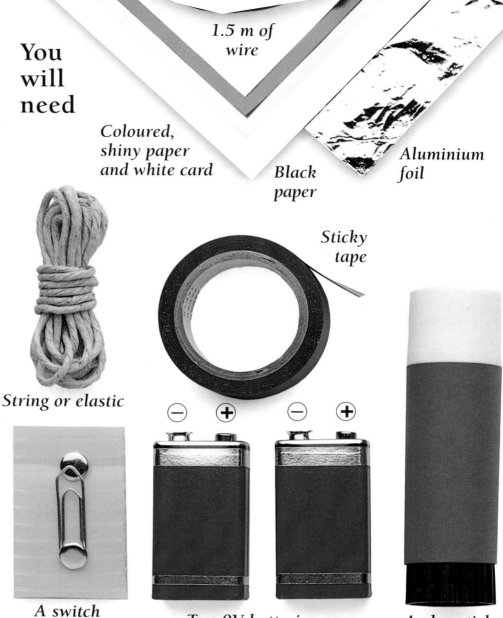

1.5 m of wire

Coloured, shiny paper and white card

Black paper

Aluminium foil

Sticky tape

String or elastic

A switch (see page 53)

Two 9V batteries

A glue stick

EQUIPMENT

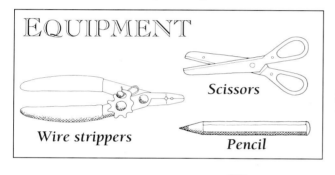

Scissors

Wire strippers

Pencil

Eight LEDs

Nuts and washers

Making the mask

1 Cut out a mask shape in black paper. Stick it on to white card. Cut slots for the eyes and the LEDs. Make holes for the string.

2 Decorate your mask with the coloured paper, washers and nuts. Thread a string through each hole and knot it, as shown.

3 Glue together a strip of paper and card, just larger than the LED slot. Make eight evenly spaced holes. Push LEDs through.

Connecting the LEDs

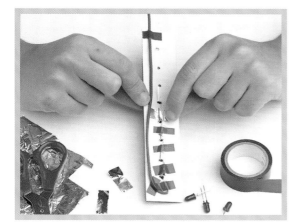

4 Bend the LEDs' legs apart*. Wrap foil tightly round the short leg of one LED and the long leg of the next, and tape them to the card. Attach one long wire to the long leg of the LED at one end of the strip of card. Attach another long wire to the short leg of the LED at the other end of the card.

5 Tape the batteries together so that the ⊕ terminal of one is next to the ⊖ of the other. Tape foil over the middle terminals.

THE GLOWING MASK
Ask someone to help you tie the string at the back of your head.

6 Connect the switch, batteries and LEDs in a circuit. Which way round do the LEDs work? Tape the LED strip to the mask.

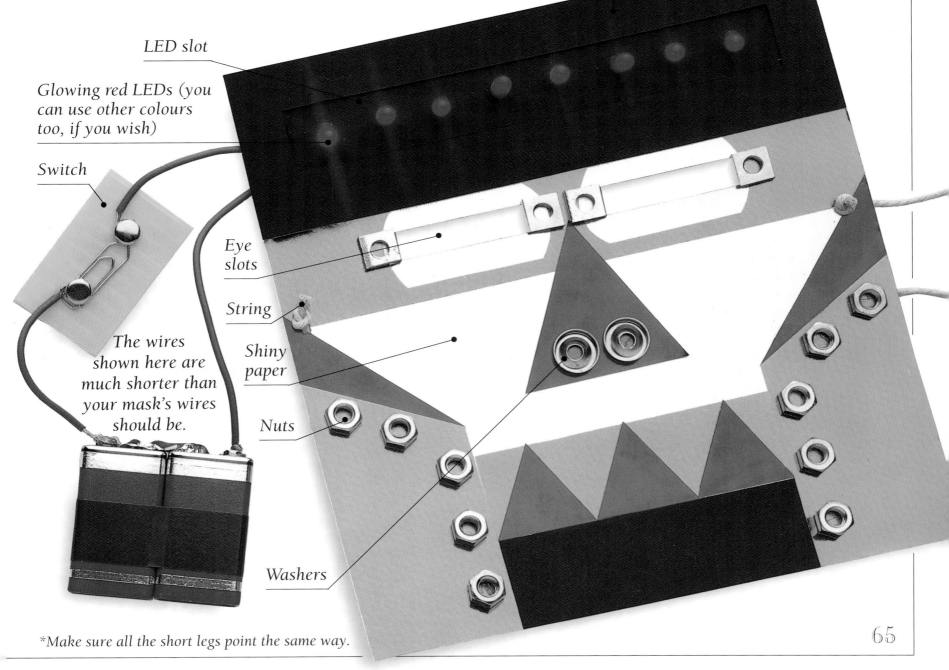

Black paper

LED slot

Glowing red LEDs (you can use other colours too, if you wish)

Switch

The wires shown here are much shorter than your mask's wires should be.

Eye slots

String

Shiny paper

Nuts

Washers

Make sure all the short legs point the same way.

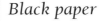

MOTOR MANIA

Electricity can do a lot more than light bulbs. If you connect a battery to an electric motor, you can make things move too! Here, and on the next two pages, you can find out how to make colourful fans to keep you cool, and a spectacular, whirling merry-go-round.

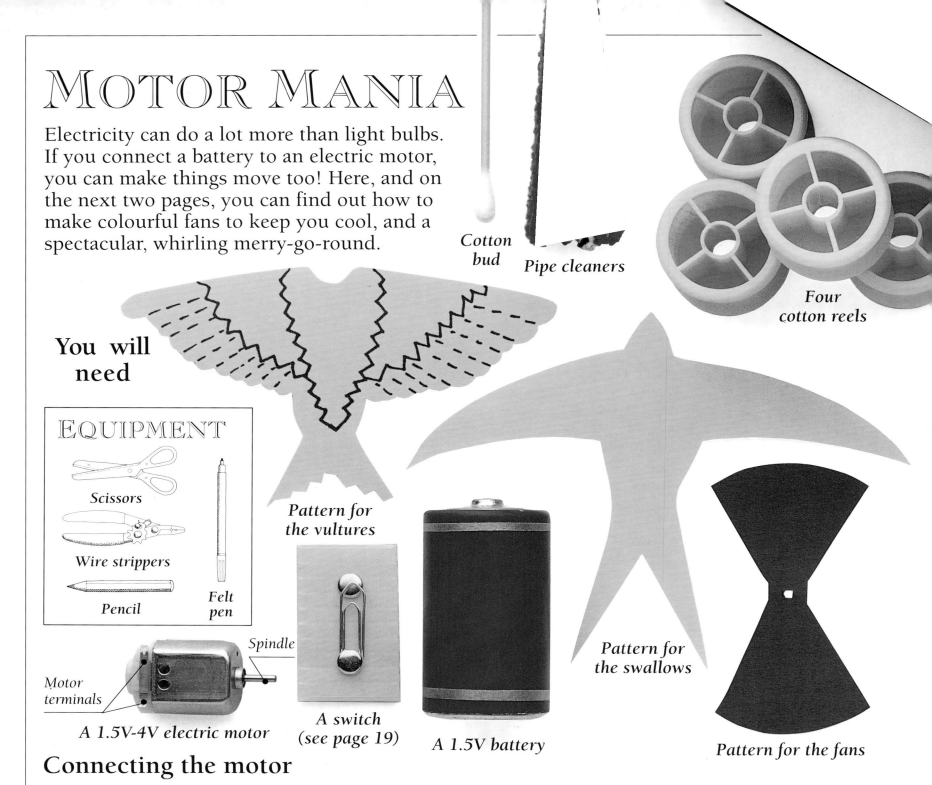

Cotton bud

Pipe cleaners

Four cotton reels

You will need

EQUIPMENT

Scissors

Wire strippers

Pencil

Felt pen

Pattern for the vultures

A switch (see page 19)

A 1.5V battery

Pattern for the swallows

Pattern for the fans

Spindle

Motor terminals

A 1.5V-4V electric motor

Connecting the motor

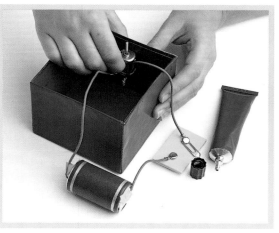

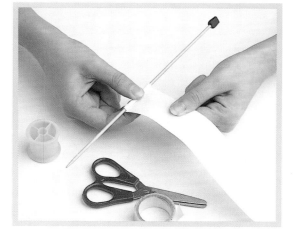

1 Connect a stripped wire to each terminal of the motor, as shown*. Cut a stem from a cotton bud. Push it on to the spindle.

2 Connect motor in a circuit, as shown. Glue the motor to the box, so that the top of the spindle is level with the top of the box.

3 To make a 'sleeve', roll a strip of paper around the knitting needle. The sleeve must fit snugly into the centre of one cotton reel.

Divide the end of the wire in half, thread one half through the terminal, then twist the two halves together.

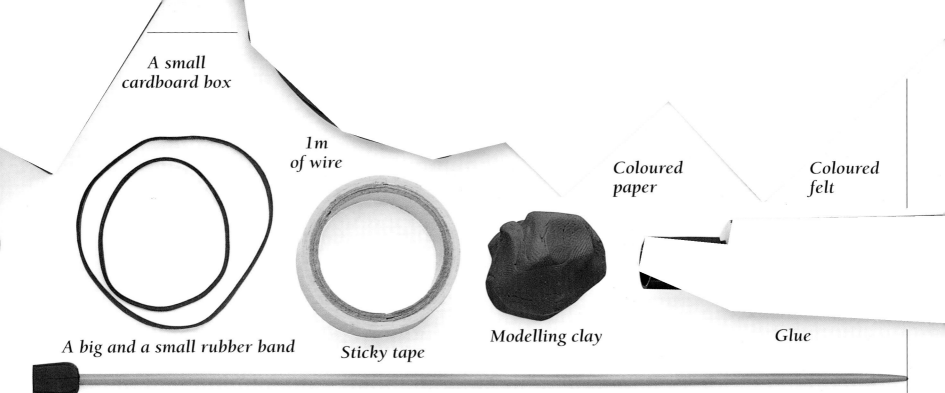

A small cardboard box

1m of wire

Coloured paper

Coloured felt

A big and a small rubber band

Sticky tape

Modelling clay

Glue

A knitting needle

Making the merry-go-round

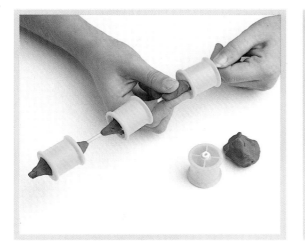

4 Stick the three other reels in place on the needle with the clay, as shown. Glue the reel with a sleeve to the bottom of the box.

5 Stretch the big rubber band round the box. Put the small band on to the reel which is third from the top of the needle, as shown.

6 Use three pipe cleaners for each bird - one for the head and body, and one for each wing. Bend vultures' heads, as shown.

7 Trace the vulture and swallow patterns, then cut them out in coloured felt. Stick the birds to the six pipe cleaner bodies with tape.

8 Tape a pipe cleaner to each bird, then tape all the birds to the top two reels, as shown. Stand the needle in the reel, in the box.

9 Glue a ring of card to the top reel. Stretch the small band on to the spindle. Make sure the tops of the motor and reel are level**

** Adjust the cotton reel with the band on it as necessary.

67

FAN-TASTIC

Making a fan

1 Use the pattern on page 66 to cut out a card fan. Make a hole in the middle of it with a pencil. Decorate it with coloured paper.

2 Connect a switch, motor, and battery together in a circuit. Push a tube cut from the stem of a cotton bud onto the motor.

3 Push the fan shape onto the spindle. Stick it in place with modelling clay. Bend the card up, as shown, to make the fan blades.

WHIRLING MERRY-GO-ROUND

Add the finishing touches to your merry-go-round by putting the battery in one corner of the box, where it won't be seen. Then, glue the switch to the outside, where you can turn it on and off easily.

Blue felt swallow

Pipe cleaner supports

Pink, blue, and yellow felt vulture

Small rubber band

IN A SPIN

As the motor runs, the spindle turns very quickly, making the small rubber band stretched between the needle and the spindle move round too. This, in turn, makes the knitting needle and merry-go-round spin.

COOL IT!

The folded blades of the fan push the air out of the way as they whizz round, producing a lovely, cooling breeze.

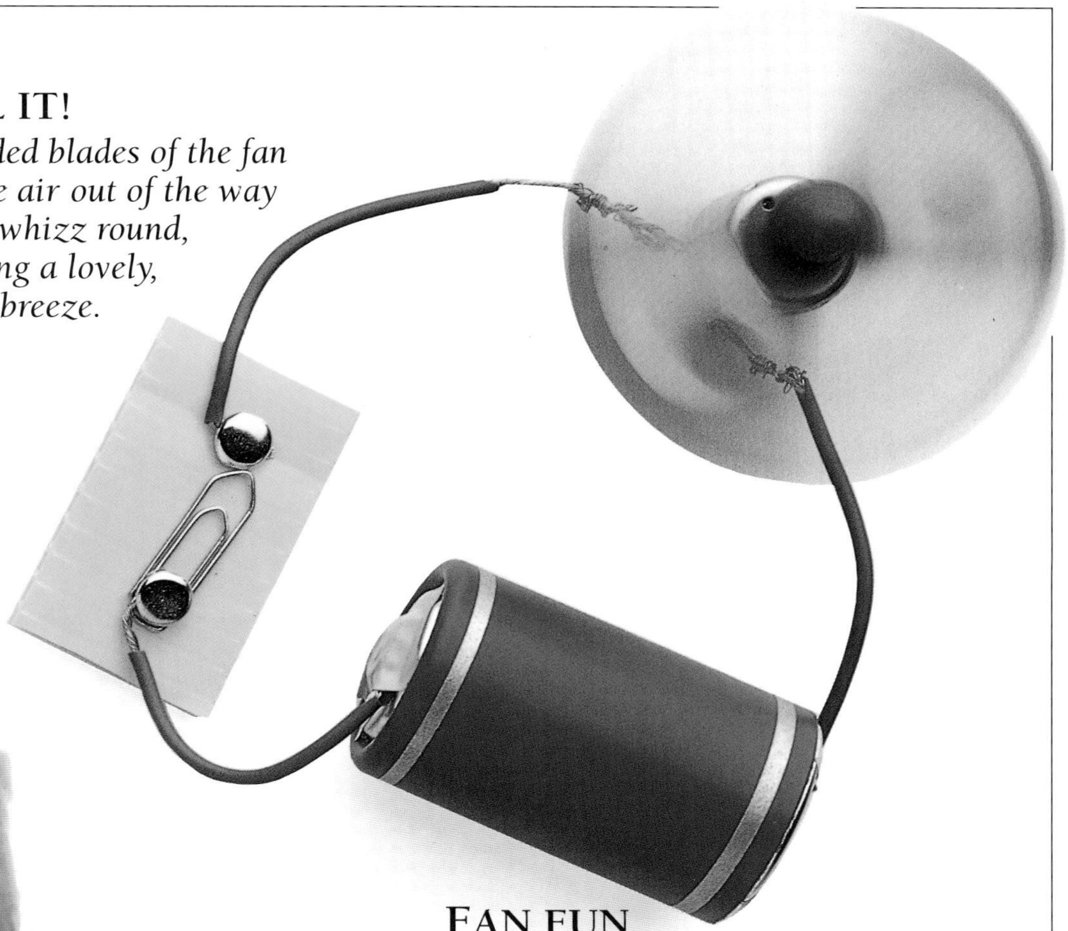

Pink and blue felt vulture

ADJUSTER

Adjust the big rubber band around the box to keep the knitting needle vertical. This will stop the small rubber band slipping off the motor.

FAN FUN

Now you have made your fan, you can start experimenting with it. Find out what happens if you connect the battery the other way round in the circuit. Try folding the fan blades up in the other direction. What happens to the amount of breeze the fan produces?

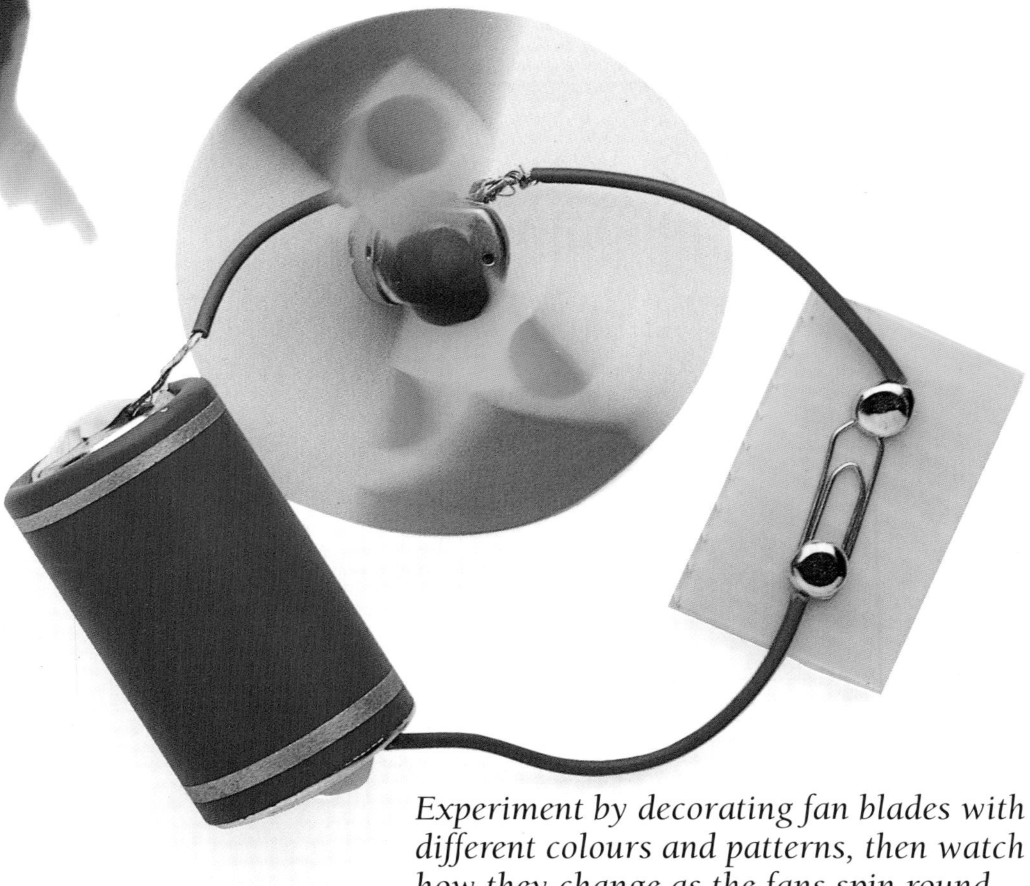

Big rubber band

Experiment by decorating fan blades with different colours and patterns, then watch how they change as the fans spin round.

69

ELECTROMAGNETS

You can make magnets with electricity, too. They are called electromagnets and, unlike ordinary magnets, their magnetic powers can be switched on and off. All you need is a battery, some wire, a screwdriver and a switch. The experiment works best if the screwdriver has an iron shaft, but a steel shaft will do.

You will need

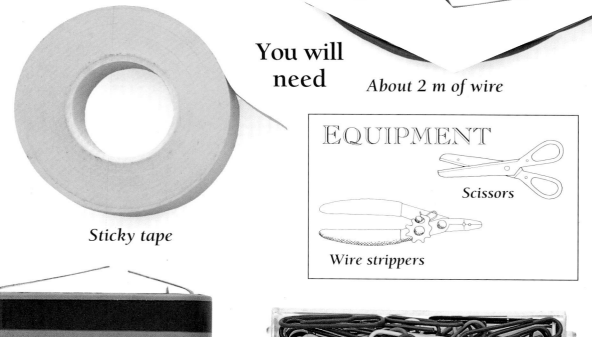
Sticky tape

About 2 m of wire

EQUIPMENT

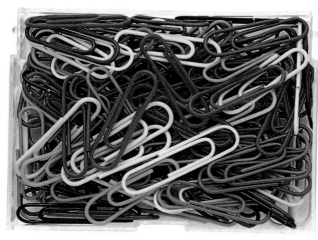
Scissors

Wire strippers

A switch (see page 53)

A 4.5V battery

Lots of paper clips

A long screwdriver

What to do

1 Strip the ends of a long piece of wire. Tape one end to the handle of a screwdriver, leaving the other end of the wire free.

2 Wind the wire tightly around the screwdriver 20, 40, or 60 times. Tape the last turn of the wire firmly to the screwdriver.

3 Connect the switch, battery, and screwdriver in a circuit, as shown. How many paper clips can each electromagnet pick up?

70

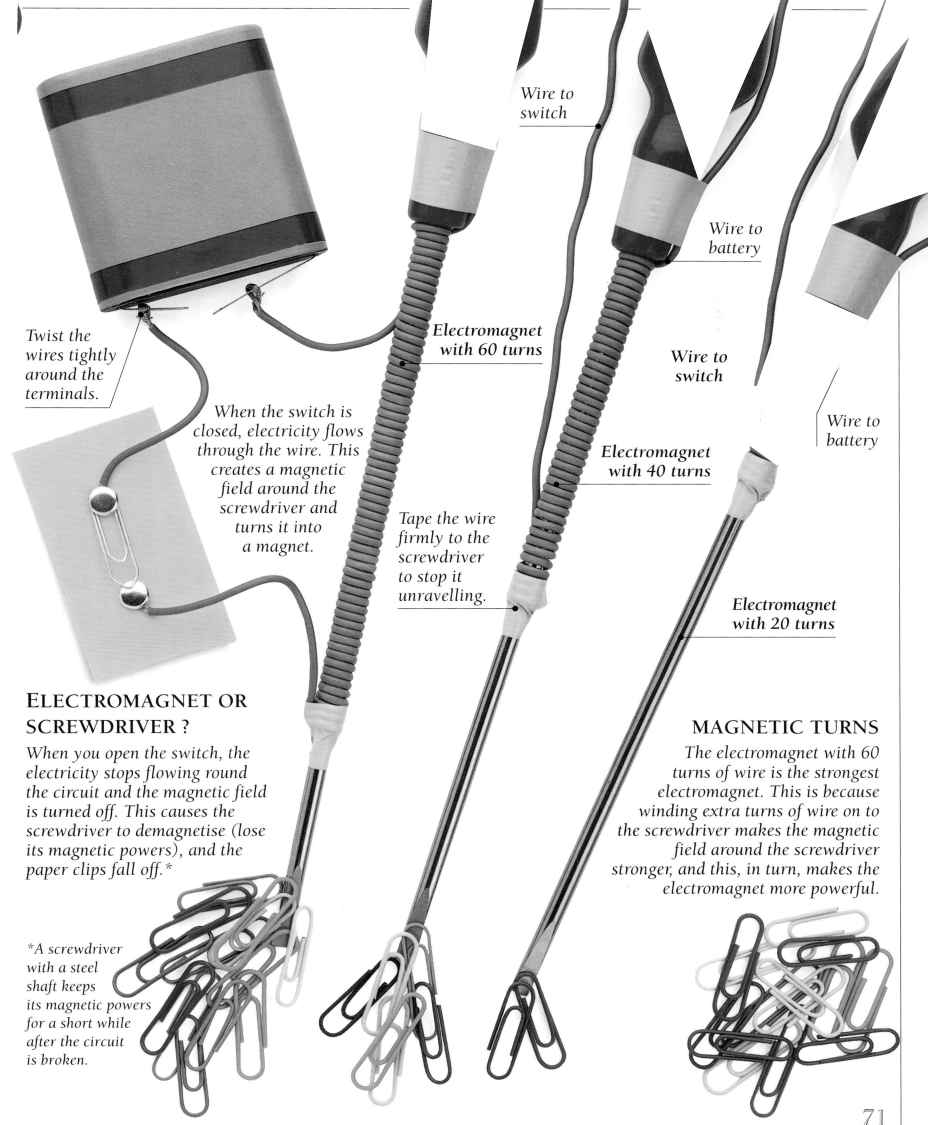

Wire to switch

Twist the wires tightly around the terminals.

Electromagnet with 60 turns

When the switch is closed, electricity flows through the wire. This creates a magnetic field around the screwdriver and turns it into a magnet.

Wire to battery

Wire to switch

Tape the wire firmly to the screwdriver to stop it unravelling.

Electromagnet with 40 turns

Wire to battery

Electromagnet with 20 turns

ELECTROMAGNET OR SCREWDRIVER ?

When you open the switch, the electricity stops flowing round the circuit and the magnetic field is turned off. This causes the screwdriver to demagnetise (lose its magnetic powers), and the paper clips fall off.*

*A screwdriver with a steel shaft keeps its magnetic powers for a short while after the circuit is broken.

MAGNETIC TURNS

The electromagnet with 60 turns of wire is the strongest electromagnet. This is because winding extra turns of wire on to the screwdriver makes the magnetic field around the screwdriver stronger, and this, in turn, makes the electromagnet more powerful.

71

BUSY BUZZER

Once you know how to make an electromagnet (see page 70), you can build this noisy buzzer. The handle of the nail-file and the paint on the drinks can don't conduct electricity, so make sure that wires are only connected to bare metal, or the buzzer won't work. Look at the photograph of the buzzer circuit, to check that you have put everything in the right place.

You will need

A 4.5V battery

A metal drinks can

Corrugated cardboard

A steel nail-file

A switch (see page 53)

Modelling clay

A cotton reel

A rubber band

Wire (at least 3 m long)

Sticky tape

An iron or steel bolt

EQUIPMENT

Scissors

Wire strippers

Making the buzzer

1 Wrap the wire firmly around the bolt 200 times. Strip both ends of the wire. Stick the bolt to the cardboard with modelling clay.

2 Attach the nail-file to the cotton reel with the rubber band, as shown. Make sure that the nail-file is held tightly in place.

3 Use the scissors to scratch away two squares of paint, along the bottom edge, on opposite sides of the drinks can.

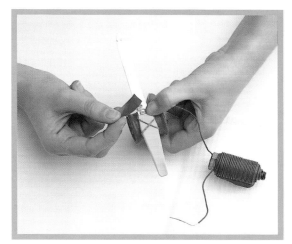

4 Firmly tape a wire from the bolt to the metal part of the nail-file, as shown. Stick the cotton reel in place on the card with clay.

5 Cut a short piece of wire and strip its ends. Attach one end to the battery. Tape the other to one of the scratched squares on the can.

6 Stick the can to the card with clay, so that the other square touches the nail-file. Connect the bolt to a switch, then to the battery.

BUZZING ABOUT

When you close the switch, electricity flows around the circuit. The bolt becomes an electromagnet and pulls the nail-file away from the can. This breaks the circuit, so that the electromagnet loses its power and the nail-file springs back, hits the can, and completes the circuit again. This process happens over and over, very quickly.

CAN-CAN
You may need to adjust the position of the can to make the buzzer work. The nail-file should just touch the scratched square on one side of the can.

The steel nail-file is attracted to the electromagnet.

FINE TUNING
Make sure that the end of the bolt is opposite the bare steel of the nail-file. If, at first, the buzzer won't work, move the cotton reel so that the nail-file is nearer to the bolt.

CONTACT!
The buzzing noise is made by the nail-file hitting the can very quickly, over and over again. Watch out for flying sparks, too!

Push the bolt firmly into the modelling clay so that the wire can't unwind.

Open the switch to stop the buzzer.

MAKING A RADIO

Have you ever wanted to make your own radio and not known where to start? Here and on the next five pages, you can find out what to do! Follow the instructions very carefully, as this project can be difficult. Everything you will need to make the radio is shown below. There are tips on where to buy the components on page 80, but don't worry if the ones you buy don't look exactly the same as the components we have used.

Corrugated cardboard

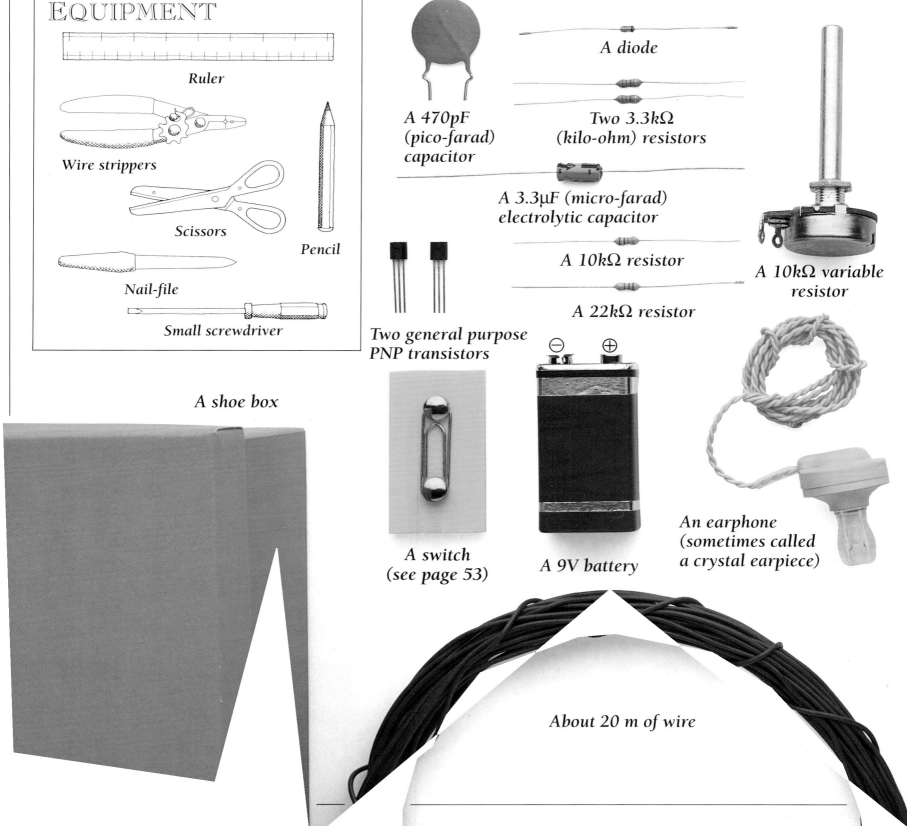

EQUIPMENT

Ruler

Wire strippers

Scissors

Pencil

Nail-file

Small screwdriver

A shoe box

You will need

A 470pF (pico-farad) capacitor

A diode

Two 3.3kΩ (kilo-ohm) resistors

A 3.3µF (micro-farad) electrolytic capacitor

A 10kΩ resistor

A 22kΩ resistor

A 10kΩ variable resistor

Two general purpose PNP transistors

⊖ ⊕

A switch (see page 53)

A 9V battery

An earphone (sometimes called a crystal earpiece)

About 20 m of wire

Preparing the box

1 Draw a rectangle, the same size as the cotton reel lying on its side, on one end of the box. Carefully cut out the rectangle.

2 Make two holes in the front of the box, as shown. The larger hole is for the volume knob, and the small one is for the earphone.

Aerial and earth wires

3 Cut out shapes from coloured paper and foil for decoration. Glue the shapes onto the box to make it look like a radio.

4 Cut one wire 10 m long, and another 5 m long. Strip one end of each wire and attach a fastener to each one.

Making a coil

5 Wrap tape, sticky-side out, round the reel. Carefully wind the fine wire onto the reel, making each turn very close to the last.

6 File the coating from one end of the fine wire and from a strip along the coil, as shown. Bend a paper clip for a tuning arm.

Aluminium foil

Coloured paper

Sticky tape

3 paper clips

2 paper fasteners

A strip of 12 screw connectors

A cotton reel

25-30 gauge magnet winding wire or resin-coated copper wire (for the receiving coil)

Glue

Radio Workshop

On the opposite page, you can see all the components connected up to make the radio circuit. Use it as a guide as you set out your circuit. The steps show you how to make each type of connection. Some components have to be connected the right way round, so if you can't tell which leg of a component is which, ask at the shop where you bought it. Turn the page to see the finished radio.

Starting off

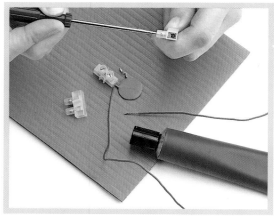

Cut a rectangle of cardboard to fit in the bottom of the box. Cut the strip of connectors into nine single blocks and one block of three.

Connecting the diode

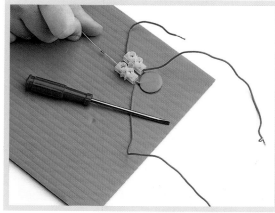

The diode must be connected the right way round in the circuit. The end with a black line is connected to the transistor.

Screw connectors

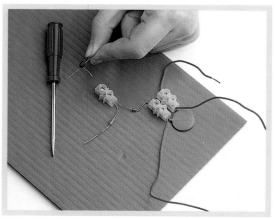

1 Partially undo the screw in one half of the screw connector. Push a wire and/or a component leg into the hole left by the screw.

Connecting transistors

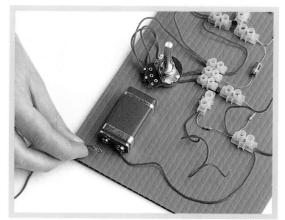

A transistor has three legs: a base, an emitter and a collector*. Bend the legs apart, as shown. Screw each leg into its connector.

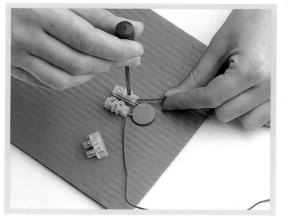

2 Wind the screw back into the connector. Check connection is firm by tugging each component. Glue the connector to the card.

Electrolytic capacitor

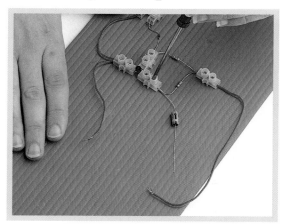

Connect the negative leg of the electrolytic capacitor (marked with an arrow or a minus sign) to the transistor's collector, as shown.

Variable resistor

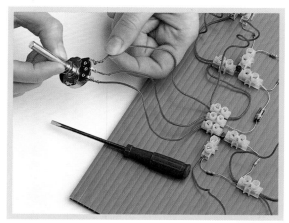

Attach one wire from each block of the three screw connectors to each of the three terminals of the variable resistor, as shown.

Connecting the battery

Make sure that the battery is connected the right way, so that the wire from the positive terminal is connected to the switch.

The instructions that come with your transistors will tell you how to find out which leg is which.

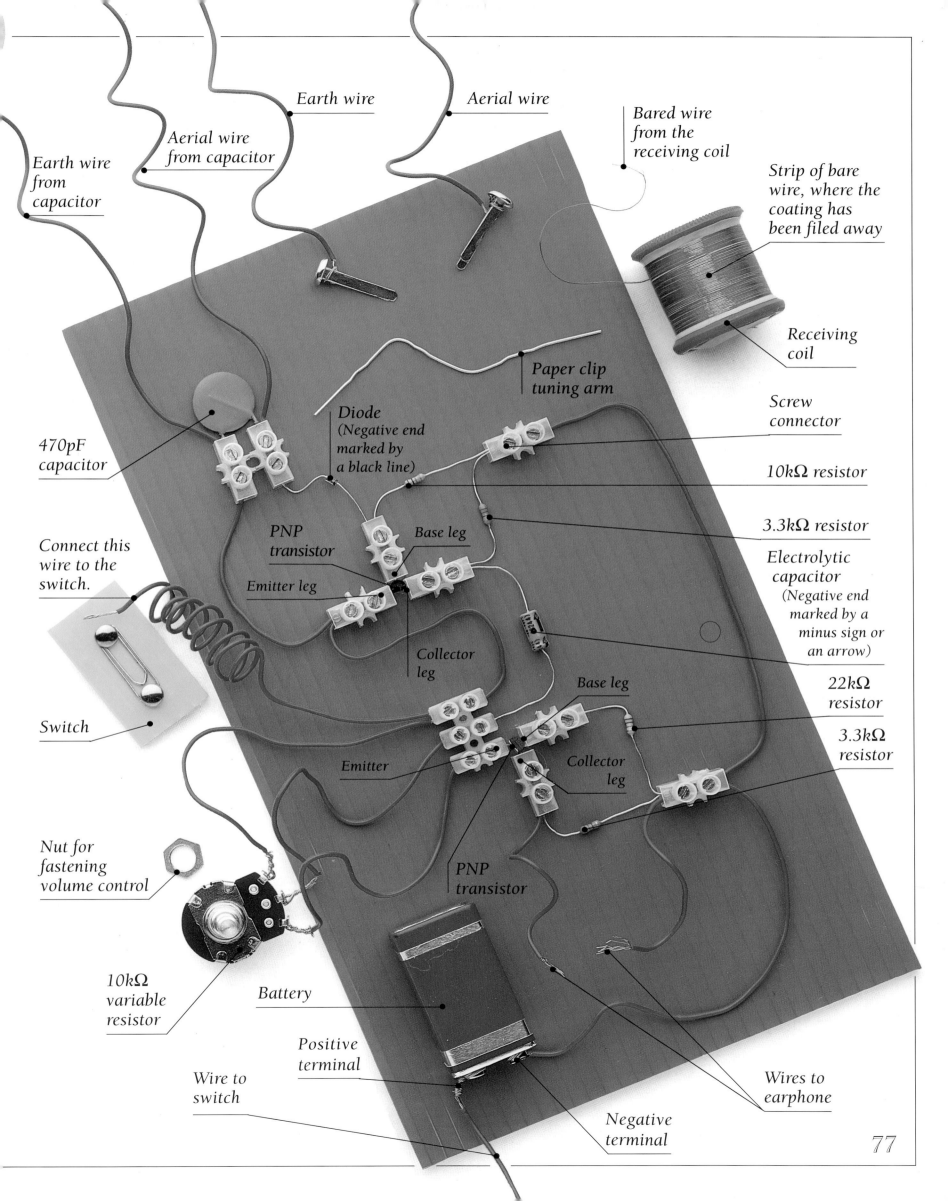

Earth wire

Aerial wire

Bared wire
from the
receiving coil

Aerial wire
from capacitor

Strip of bare
wire, where the
coating has
been filed away

Earth wire
from
capacitor

Receiving
coil

470pF
capacitor

Paper clip
tuning arm

Screw
connector

Diode
(Negative end
marked by
a black line)

10kΩ resistor

3.3kΩ resistor

Base leg

PNP
transistor

Electrolytic
capacitor
(Negative end
marked by a
minus sign or
an arrow)

Connect this
wire to the
switch.

Emitter leg

Collector
leg

22kΩ
resistor

3.3kΩ
resistor

Switch

Base leg

Emitter

Collector
leg

Nut for
fastening
volume control

PNP
transistor

10kΩ
variable
resistor

Battery

Wires to
earphone

Positive
terminal

Wire to
switch

Negative
terminal

ON THE AIR

Finishing off

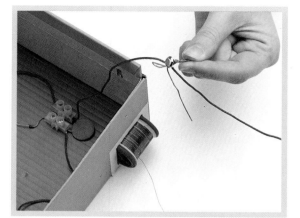

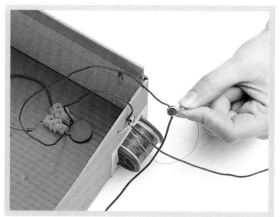

1 Put the circuit into the box. Tape the coil halfway through the hole so that the bared wire and the filed strip are outside the box.

2 Bend the tuning arm around the earth wire's paper fastener, as shown. Attach the earth wire from the capacitor to the paper fastener.

3 Attach the capacitor's aerial wire and coil's bare wire to the aerial wire's paper fastener. Push fasteners through box, as below.

Tuning the radio

Once you have finished making the radio, you are ready to tune in to the airwaves! First, put the earphone in your ear, very carefully. Then, move the tuning arm slowly along the bare wire of the receiving coil to tune in to different radio stations. The more turns of wire there are on the coil, the more radio stations you will be able to pick up.

Wire from receiving coil to aerial wire

Paper clip tuning-arm

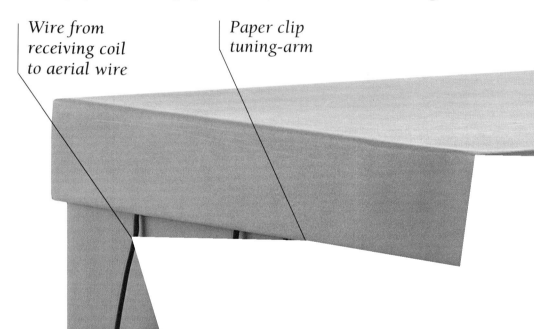

Switch

AERIAL

The aerial works best when it is hung in the air in a straight line, with some of it out of doors. This way, it can catch as much of the radio signal as possible.

EARTH WIRE

Strip 15 cm of plastic from the end of the earth wire, then attach the end to a metal tap in a sink.

Bend the tuning arm so that it touches the bared wire of the coil, very firmly.

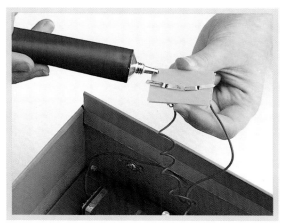

4 Connect the spare wire from the battery to the switch. Glue the switch to the outside of the box, beside the receiving coil.

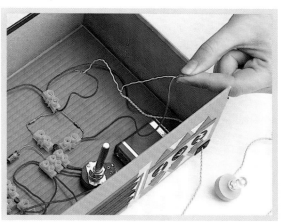

5 Push both earphone wires through the hole in the box. Connect one of them to each of the free wires from the 3.3kΩ resistor.

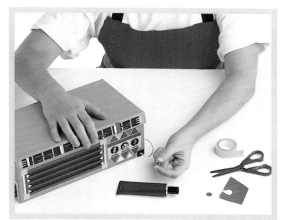

6 Push the variable resistor arm through its hole and screw the nut on tightly. Wind tape round the knob, as shown, to decorate it.

Turn the volume knob up for very quiet stations.

Troubleshooting

You should be able to tune in to a few radio stations using your radio. The sound will be faint, but you should be able to hear what the announcer is saying or what music is playing. If your radio does not seem to work, make sure you check all the connections: just one wire or component leg that is not connecting will mean that the radio will not work. Make sure that the diode, the transistors, the capacitor and the battery are all connected the right way round. Ask an adult to help you.

Push the earphone wire back into the box when you finish listening to the radio.

LISTENING IN

The invisible radio waves, which carry the signals of radio stations through the air, are made of electricity and magnetism! They are picked up by the radio's aerial. Tuning the radio selects the signal from one radio station and makes it stronger. The earphone changes the signal into sound, so that you can hear it.

CIRCUIT CHECKLIST

If you have any problems getting your electrical circuits to work, try checking the following things:

1 Always check that you have connected each component and wire of the circuit exactly as you have been shown.

2 Make sure that connections made with tape or kitchen foil are tight enough, by pressing them together firmly.

3 Check that no component, foil connection, or stray wire in one part of the circuit is touching another part by accident, as the electricity will miss out components or maybe even the whole circuit. This problem is called a short-circuit.

4 If a circuit stays on when the switch is open, make sure that the paper fasteners are not touching underneath the switch.

5 If you have checked all of the above, and your circuit still doesn't work, try replacing the batteries.

6 If your circuit still doesn't work, one or more of the components could be faulty. In the radio, this is most likely to be the transistors. Try replacing them.

SUPPLIERS

If you have trouble finding any of the components or equipment needed for projects in this book, try contacting the suppliers suggested below.

Hardware or General Electrical Shops - screwdrivers, wire strippers, wire, batteries, motors, bulb holders, bulbs, magnets, strip connectors, nuts, bolts, washers.
Electronics Components Shops/Suppliers (Try electronics shops or television repairers, or look in the phone book and electronics magazines for names and addresses of local suppliers) - components for the radio, wire, hook-up wire, LEDs.
Model and Craft Shops - motors, felt, pipe cleaners, corrugated plastic.
Toy Shops - iron filings, magnets.